UNLIKELY HEROES

UNLIKELY HEROES

How God uses imperfect people

Peter Read

Inter-Varsity Press

INTER-VARSITY PRESS

38 De Montfort Street, Leicester LE1 7GP, England

First published 1990

British Library Cataloguing in Publication Data
Read, Peter
  Unlikely heroes.
  1. Bible. O.T. Characters
  I. Title
  221.922

ISBN 0-85110-837-7

Set in Baskerville

Typeset in Great Britain by Avocet Robinson, Buckingham

Printed and bound in Great Britain by
Courier International Ltd, Tiptree, Essex

*Inter-Varsity Press is the book-publishing division of the Universities and
Colleges Christian Fellowship (formerly the Inter-Varsity Fellowship), a
student movement linking Christian Unions in universities and colleges
throughout the United Kingdom and the Republic of Ireland, and a member
movement of the International Fellowship of Evangelical Students. For
information about local and national activities write to UCCF,
38 De Montfort Street, Leicester LE1 7GP.*

CONTENTS

The Preacher   7

1   Men of failure, men of faith   11

2   Gideon the inferior   15

3   Barak the hesitant   34

4   Samson the flippant   49

5   Jephthah the rash   71

6   David and his loves   89

7   Samuel: the faithful child and
      hesitant man   118

8   One faith, many failures?   142

9   A minister looks around   153

List of Bible passages used   159

The Preacher

The preacher's fist hit the lectern hard. The glass wobbled, the water spilt. 'God's people,' he shouted, 'must be other-worldly.' He stared at the congregation, then, with bulging eyes seeming to fill his entire face, he shared a little story. 'Yesterday the local football team had a big cup-match. Thousands of people went to watch.' His voice lowered; we almost expected some relief from the thundering of the past twenty minutes. We were soon to be disappointed.

He continued, building up into another ear-splitting crescendo. 'The people were chanting their heroes' names. I know, I heard them as I drove past. They were praising ordinary men. God is not pleased with that kind of behaviour.' Then, in time to hammering fist and shuddering glass, he shouted 'Sad to relate, some of God's people were there.'

I gulped and returned his stare. I was one of God's people who had been cheering the local lads the previous day. Or at least, I thought I was one of God's people. As the sermon progressed I began to wonder. We were told that Christians should not mix with unbelievers and they should never fail in anything they attempted for God. The thundering preacher paraded his thundering God, well pleased with Abraham, Moses, David and the like, but not too pleased with 'miserable worms of the dunghill' such as myself, who had been elated by the last-gasp winner the previous day.

That juvenile feeling of being an inferior Christian persisted for many years. Conversations with others confirmed my suspicion that many Christians felt the same way. They too looked at Christian biographies brimming with success. Pages crammed with healings and multiple conversions all had the effect of making them feel uncomfortable about their own Christian lives, filled as they were with countless failures. Other Christians were not much help. They seemed wiser, more dynamic and more effective in evangelism. Prayer meetings, in which they sent lengthy and wordy offerings to the throne of grace, reduced me to a self-conscious gibbering wreck when it was my turn to pray.

Bible studies and sermons failed to alleviate my fears. Bible characters were portrayed in the pulpit as people who never got it wrong. We were back to the modern Christian biographies – all success and no mistakes. Sermons reinforced the stories. Three, or sometimes more, alliterated points of application told me that if I really were a Christian then I should be holy in my actions, thoughts and deeds. Occasional preachers tried to help by reminding me that God is a forgiving God who knows that I am weak and will fail. But such hope was like a drop in the ocean. The whole weight of Christian exposition suggested that my Christian life was in ruins and that I should be more successful in everything I did.

Then one day I stumbled across Hebrews 11, a passage celebrating people of faith from Old Testament times. The chapter resounds to those who left everything they possessed in the hope of finding a heavenly city. They were people who believed in a God they could not see; who faced death with confidence because of the reality of their hope. People who stopped the mouths of lions, conquered kingdoms, raised people from the dead, quenched the fury of the flames and escaped the edge of the sword.

At first sight such a passage does little to restore confidence in the flagging faith of a young Christian. Closer examination, however, reveals that they all had weaknesses . . .

Peter Read

CHAPTER ONE

MEN OF FAILURE, MEN OF FAITH

'And what more shall I say? I do not have time to tell about Gideon, Barak, Samson, Jephthah, David, Samuel and the prophets, who through faith conquered kingdoms, administered justice, and gained what was promised; who shut the mouths of lions, quenched the fury of the flames, and escaped the edge of the sword; whose weakness was turned to strength; and who became powerful in battle and routed foreign armies. Women received back their dead, raised to life again. Others were tortured and refused to be released, so that they might gain a better resurrection. Some faced jeers and flogging, while still others were chained and put in prison. They were stoned; they were sawn in two; they were put to death by the sword. They went about in sheepskins and goatskins, destitute, persecuted and ill-treated – the world was not worthy of them. They wandered in deserts and mountains, and in caves and holes in the ground. These were all commended for their faith, yet none of them received what had been promised.'

(Hebrews 11:32–39)

Abraham, Noah, Moses and Jacob all had parts to their history of which they were ashamed. The final section of the chapter in Hebrews recalls the exploits of six individuals. Whilst the author of Hebrews has run out of time to offer detailed character studies, it is of these men he makes the remarks you have just read. Gideon, Barak, Samson, Jephthah, David and Samuel. Yet careful study of these men reveals that they all failed.

Gideon was an inferior, constantly aware of his own background and family. Even when God was real to him, he wanted assurances that it really was God.

Barak hesitated time and again. Afraid of going by himself against the enemy, he told God, point blank, he would only go if accompanied by Deborah. His reign as judge was marred by an inability to rally all the tribes to the cause.

Gideon and Barak, for all their mistakes, appear saints by the side of Samson. He systematically broke all of his vows to God, and his whole life was dominated by a flirtatious spirit. Three disastrous relationships, one of them with a prostitute, led to his ultimate demise. In between his rumbustious dealings in Timnah and Gaza, he managed to upset his parents, isolate the people he was sent to deliver, and intimidate the Philistines into a wholesale policy of violent vengeance.

Jephthah's credentials were not the sort to please a respectable Western evangelical church. A bandit leader of a group of desperadoes in the hill country of Tob, he was called to be a judge of Israel after the elders had seen his exploits with his motley group of adventurers. He had fled to Tob because his half-brothers had conspired against him. Aware that he was the illegitimate son of a relationship between their father and a prostitute, they were unhappy at the thought that he might inherit the family wealth.

Because of this, they actually forced him out of his home.

David, for all his attributes on the battlefield and his spiritual sensitivity in penning many of the Psalms, was a man whose sensuality led to difficulties both for himself and his nation.

Samuel, the leader of God's people, was a man whose hesitancy and caution caused many difficulties.

It is these people who are applauded in the letter to the Hebrews as men of faith. The writer offers a clue as he explains that their weaknesses were turned to strength. Such characters remind us that God uses human vessels to do his work on earth. They also remind us that they were effective only as long as they sought God's help. God accepts us 'warts and all', and is quite capable of using people who do not always match our carefully-devised manuals on 'The Ideal Christian Leader.'

Such people also remind us of the diversity of Christian leaders. Samson was different from Gideon who in turn was different from David. Hebrews 11 concludes the list of unsung heroes with a reference to the prophets. They were totally different. Isaiah was a stately prophet who had access to the king's court. Amos was a farmer who did not even like the term prophet. Jeremiah was a self-conscious youngster who on one occasion felt he would rather die than proclaim God's message. Ezekiel was an extrovert who was not afraid of performing symbolic parables in front of the people. Hosea was a prophet who shared the intense hurt of his own broken marriage as a picture of the grief and love of God for faithless Israel. Such sensitivity seems to be lacking in the preaching of Amos, whose stinging sermons often attacked and destroyed Israel's complacency.

The diversity of these people of faith reminds us that there is no such thing as a stereotype Christian leader. Yet, many ordinary Christians feel they have to dress, react and speak in a certain way before they can be accepted. Such behaviour forgets that God respects our unique personality and while he will adapt and change it, he will never allow it to be obliterated.

The themes of the ordinariness, diversity and failure of these six men of faith are the concern of this book. It is not intended as a celebration of failure and sin. Rather, it is offered as a reminder that it was God who equipped this motley crew to achieve such great things. It is this God who still promises to transform our weakness into his strength, as he did for Gideon, Barak, Samson, Jephthah, David, and Samuel. As we examine their faith we will do it through re-telling their stories as we find them in the Old Testament. And so we call contributor number one; Gideon the inferior. He comes to tell his story and our story. A story of failure and faith.

CHAPTER TWO

GIDEON
THE INFERIOR

(JUDGES 6–8)

Reflections *(Judges 6:1 – 10)*

He loved this scene. In front of him the valleys rolling and stretching as far as the eye could see. Behind, the winepress, and above that, the crags where he had played as a boy.

He felt childhood joy as he recalled endless hot days when they carried grapes into the labyrinth of caves. He could hear again the enduring songs of kinsmen and children as they crushed fruit into a red gooey river of wine.

Today, the view evoked different emotions. A mixture of anger and frustration filled him as his gaze took in the empty slopes and desolate homesteads. Sheep, cattle and donkeys no longer peppered the fields. Everywhere was an eerie emptiness. For seven years his land had been ravaged by the Midianites. Glancing behind, he could just make out the shapes of four or five people. There were many more huddled into clefts of rocks, cramming possessions, animals and bedding into whatever nook or cranny they could find.

As he threshed the wheat, he hummed some of the songs of his youth. It was painful to recall how little singing he had heard lately. His people were dispirited and divided. There was little scope for large scale celebrations. People were too frightened of the Midianites to leave their mountain refuge. He thought of the words he sang; songs his father Joash had taught him. They were all full of praise to Jehovah. Jehovah: the God who had led his people out of bondage and crushed the might of Pharaoh and Egypt. Why, Gideon wondered, was he so silent now?

True, a man had recently appeared in Israel claiming he was a prophet sent from the God of heaven. He had argued that Israel was suffering because they had failed to honour God throughout their history. Some of the people had listened to his message and had prayed earnestly to God for his intervention. As far as Gideon was concerned it begged more questions than it answered. Why was this God so angry? Why hadn't he been rather more apparent in their recent history? For seven years they had struggled against the Midianites. As the wind carried away the chaff, Gideon glanced at the remaining wheat. It was a pitiful crop. They had left very little for him or anyone else this year.

Something would have to be done. But what? And by whom? Jehovah was silent. Even his father's other gods had been impotent in delivering the people. Joash was in charge of the shrine for Baal and the grove dedicated to Asherah. But for some reason, even three gods had been unable to help Gideon's people.

They desperately needed another leader to rally the people and banish the enemy: a man with a combination of militaristic strategy and spiritual insight. Unfortunately,

Moses-style characters were in short supply in Israel. There must surely be someone, somewhere. As long as no-one asked Gideon to go. He was a nobody, unimportant in his family, eclipsed by his rather dominating father. Besides, their family was fairly low down in the batting order when it came to his tribe. And even his tribe was unimportant compared with the other rather impressive Israelite groupings. Among all of those people there must be one potential leader. He would carry on threshing the wheat and keeping out of the way of marauding Midianites until they found such an individual.

God's assessment *(Judges 6:11–24)*

The man made Gideon jump. He hadn't noticed him arrive and didn't know how long he had been sitting under the tree. His opening words were rather strange: 'The Lord is with you, mighty warrior.' It was uncanny – almost as though the stranger knew exactly what Gideon had been thinking over the past few moments. His mutterings and murmurings against silent Jehovah were being exposed. It was as though he had been holding a conversation with the man who was now correcting some of Gideon's inaccuracies. The Lord *is* with you, young man.

Gideon wasn't sure who this stranger was, but he would give him a piece of his mind. So God was with them was he? Of course, Gideon would honour the rules of Jewish politeness, but even so . . .

'But sir,' Gideon replied, 'if the Lord is with us, why has all this happened to us? Where are all his wonders that our fathers told us about when they said "Did not the Lord bring us up out of Egypt?" But now the Lord has abandoned us and put us into the hand of Midian.'

He felt a little better for being able to express these deep

17

feelings of frustration. Only as the stranger turned and faced him did Gideon feel uneasy. Who exactly was he? Could he possibly be a messenger from God's presence?

It was not only his guest's appearance which unsettled Gideon, but also the deep authority of his speech. He had begun the conversation by assuring Gideon that God was with him and that Gideon was a mighty man of valour. The stranger then went on to inform Gideon that he was commissioning him to be the deliverer of Israel. There was no need to be afraid because he would be with Gideon and would help him to strike down the Midianites.

This was wonderful fighting talk. The type of thing Gideon had longed for at the winepress. But Gideon had convinced himself he was not the man for the job. This uninvited guest assumed there was no-one else! It was time for one or two questions.

They rolled off Gideon's lips. How could he save Israel? Didn't this stranger know his inferiority problems? Wasn't he aware of the low status of his tribe in Israel? As his guest continued, more questions were shaped. It was all very well saying the Midianites would be crushed by the power and presence of God working in Gideon. Here at the tree in Ophrah such talk was impressive and easy. There wasn't a Midianite or one of their hated camels in sight. But what would happen when he had left and the task was completely in Gideon's hands? Would he be so certain that this conversation had been with the living God? Would he later think the heat and the threshing had invoked an hallucination?

It was such confused thoughts that forced Gideon to question the identity of the messenger.

'If now I have found favour in your sight,' he said, 'give me a sign that it really is you talking to me.'

The sign was impressive by any standards. The meat and bread which Gideon had prepared were placed on a rock. The visitor touched them with the tip of his staff. Fire raged and consumed them in seconds. The visitor, too, was gone. As quietly, as quickly as he had come. So this really had been God's messenger. And Gideon was really being commissioned to rally Israel and lead them against Midian. But wait a minute! Hadn't Gideon heard his father tell how Moses was terrified of looking into the face of God? Didn't every Jew know that God's holiness was so intense that no human being could ever stand in his presence? Such presumption would end in death. Gideon wasn't as righteous as Moses and yet not only had he stood in God's presence, he had made a meal for him and even argued with him.

'Ah, Sovereign Lord,' he prayed with real earnestness, 'I have seen the angel of the Lord face to face.'

The voice reassured him: 'Peace! Do not be afraid. You are not going to die.'

Gideon felt entirely different. His whole body tingled. He was a strange mixture of every imaginable emotion: he was excited about the prospects of delivering Israel, humbled that the living God had come to him of all people, terrified about his own inabilities and weaknesses and joyful because God had not abandoned his people. As all these different feelings tumbled through his consciousness there was one emotion which seemed to hold and control them all. He felt a deep peace. A peace he had never felt before. In the past he had only experienced the deep impotence which comes from frustration and inferiority. Now he knew that God was with him.

He wanted to mark this spot, not just for himself but for future generations, so that he could tell his children's children 'This is where I met the living God.' And so he built an altar and called it, naturally enough, 'The Lord is peace.'

As he selected the stones and fitted them into shape, he recalled the recent meeting and felt again the invigorating sense of God. He remembered his promises. The promise of his presence; that during any future bout of inferiority Gideon must remember it is his God who is sending him. He remembered, too, the power of God. The spectacular display of that power on the rock, and the promise that he would crush Midian. And as the altar took shape, he remembered and began to feel, even now, the reality of God's promise of peace.

The monstrosity on the hill *(Judges 6:25–32)*

Gideon's peace was soon to be severely tested. After filling him with his power, the promise of his presence and his peace, God was next to expose him to fear. It was as if he was saying 'Yes, you feel at peace with me here at the altar with all its memories of your spiritual experience; now let's see how real that peace is.'

The task sounded straightforward enough. On the hill above the village was an altar to Baal the Canaanite god and a pole for Asherah. Gideon was to dismantle and smash both. Of course, there would be danger involved. The altar was owned and protected by his father. The villagers, who had grown to trust in the Canaanite deities as well as Jehovah, would be outraged when they discovered what had happened. Their superstition would lead to mass panic and fear and they could certainly demand the death of the culprit. Gideon was going to need his God-given peace!

It was not only his new found peace which God wanted to test. Through the prophet God had already communicated his displeasure at Israel's disloyalty. How could this new deliverer pretend to be aware of God's constant presence and yet worship him along with one or two other gods? God was calling him to make a decisive act in front of his family. His private sense of God's presence was being forced into the open. God was demanding that he should realize that his presence was not just a reassuring emotion but it was also exclusive. God would be with him in all his endeavours, but he would not cohabit with other gods. The call to destroy the altar was a call to publicly affirm that God was his God.

The day gave way to night-fall and the monstrosities were still on the hill. No doubt God wanted a mid-afternoon performance (as, one day, Elijah would challenge the prophets of Baal on Mount Carmel). Gideon did not want to do the deed during such peak viewing time. He took ten men and stealthily dismantled the altar and pole in the thick of night. Of course, where gossip is concerned, ten men in a small community is a large number. It wasn't long before the outraged villagers knew exactly who was responsible.

God, who had promised his presence, fulfilled his promise in the ensuing events. Gideon ended up with an unlikely advocate. Repeatedly during his night-time escapade he must have imagined the pained and angry expression on the face of his father, Joash. Yet, remarkably, it was he who defended his son by saying 'If Baal really is a god, he can defend himself when someone breaks down his altar.'

In less than twenty-four hours, Gideon had moved from the relative security of threshing wheat at the winepress to facing death twice: once in his face to face encounter with God's messenger and then in the violent responses of his kinsfolk. The man of faith had started on his long trek forward. He was learning that peace, power and divine presence were not three compartmentalized experiences closeting him from reality. They were given to him for the rough and tumble of life, and will bring him repeatedly to stare death in the face. Peace in the Christian experience is inevitably followed by fear in order to test its authenticity.

An encounter with the Spirit of God *(Judges 6:33–40)*

'Then the spirit of the Lord clothed himself in Gideon' (verse 34).

After the incident on the hill and Joash's intervention, the people of the district renamed Gideon. They called him Jerub Baal which means 'let Baal contend'. A man who has been definitely called and set aside for God's task, is still affected by a pagan culture. Despite his action against the altar and cultish pole, he was still carrying around with him a name celebrating Baal rather than Jehovah. We will never know whether Joash and his family totally repudiated pagan practices. Future events suggest they were still heavily influenced by such beliefs.

God's man of faith represents two warring cultures. The one immersed in fertility rites, superstition and syncretism, the other symbolized by an uncompromising commitment to the monotheistic belief (the belief that there is only one God).

Clearly, with such a man there is a need for a definite work of God. Such a work is celebrated by the writer of Judges when he informs us that the 'Spirit of God clothed himself in Gideon'. The God of heaven who is depicted throughout Scripture as an unseen spirit, suddenly clothes himself in the form of an unlikely human hero. The people, many of whom must have shared Gideon's Ophrah feelings that God had abandoned his people, would now be left in no doubt that this God would be working for them. His Spirit was going to wrap himself around Gideon in such

22

a way that no longer would an onlooker see an inferior individual from an obscure tribe, but instead would glimpse the living God operating through his Spirit in the everyday exploits of Gideon.

That such an outpouring of God's Spirit occurred for Gideon is clear from the fact that he changed instantly from a hesitant individual. Instead he sounded the trumpet and called his fellow Abiezrites to follow him. Later, he would give them the rousing slogan 'For God and for Gideon.' He knew where his strength resided but at the same time he could now cope with his changed personality. He was no longer an inferior cowering in a winepress, or paranoid with fear that he would die because of a divine encounter. The Spirit of God was mysteriously clothed in him and willing to express himself through his acts. So, with no apology, Gideon blew the trumpet, sent messages to Manasseh, Zebulun and Naphtali and would later tell them to fight for God and Gideon.

The two themes of this book – faith and failure – have been pointed out already. In every man and woman of God they work hand in hand, inextricably mixed together. In Gideon, like all the other characters we will study, there was no Hollywood-style movement from black to white. We have charted his movement from doubt to Spirit-inspired power. It is a great temptation to draw the curtain on his life and proclaim that he and his offspring lived happily ever after. Yet the Bible writers would preclude such a statement. After the clarion trumpet-call encouraging the troops to rally for God and for Gideon, he had his first major attack of fear.

Perhaps the fear mounted when he saw the response. If no-one had responded he could have consoled himself with the fact that he was too insignificant for such a major task. After all, hadn't he said as much to the angel at

Ophrah? But now, this huge assembling army made him feel vulnerable. The tribesmen of Manasseh, Asher, Zebulun and Naphtali arrived throughout the day. On one level, of course, it was consoling to have so many rallying to the cause. On the other hand, each man reinforced the fact that he was looking to Gideon for leadership. It was no doubt this thought which prompted him to talk with God. He had felt full of courage when sending out the invitations and blowing his trumpet. Somehow it is easy to feel confident about a project when it's still in the future. Thirty-two thousand potential fighters were now saying the project must be moved from the pending to the urgent action tray. There was no chance of turning back. Yet the doubts were surfacing again. He needed to be doubly sure that God would really deliver the Israelites.

He woke early the next morning to see whether God had kept his side of the bargain. He had placed a fleece in the entrace to the winepress late the previous evening. If the fleece was wet and the rest of the ground dry, then he would know that God was with him and would destroy the Midianites and deliver the Israelites. As he climbed the path to the winepress, he touched the ground. It was bone dry. He approached the mouth of the cave full of excitement. Yes. The fleece was sodden. So God had heard. God was on his side. God would deliver Israel through Gideon.

Before the hoorahs and hallejuahs had time to surface, another horrible doubt was appearing in Gideon's mind. Just supposing the soaking fleece was a natural phenomenon. What if it had soaked up all the dew? Perhaps it was nothing to do with God after all. Gideon needed to know. But wouldn't God be angry? He had been so long-suffering with him up to this point, there was surely a danger of a divine 'enough's enough' statement. But

Gideon couldn't lead the troops with this niggling thought gnawing away at him. So it was with some trepidation that he approached God for the second time in twenty-four hours. The new plan would satisfy Gideon's mounting doubts. 'Do not be angry with me,' he said. 'Let me make just one more request. Allow me one more test with the fleece. This time make the fleece dry and the ground covered with dew.' That would be some miracle! So God did it. And Gideon rallied the troops at the spring of Harod, ready for action. But God wasn't quite finished with him yet!

Who's in charge? *(Judges 7:1–25)*

Three momentous incidents had confirmed for Gideon that God was with him. The fire on the rock at Ophrah had demonstrated the divine power at his disposal. The sensation of the Spirit of God sweeping through him had enabled him to rally his kinsmen with confidence. (It had also reminded him that he was not being asked to do this work in his own strength. God was going to clothe himself in Gideon.) The experience with the fleece reminded Gideon that God would be patient with him through the forthcoming enterprise.

There was always a danger that, once he had reached the other side of these incidents, Gideon would grow in the wrong kind of confidence. It would be easy for him to feel that his inferiority was now a thing of the past and that thirty-two thousand men respected and looked up to him for leadership.

It may have been to prevent Gideon and the Israelites feeling this way that God contacted him with his plan. As far as God was concerned, Gideon had too many men. He was to throw out a general challenge. If anyone was trembling with fear he must leave at once. It sounded eminently sensible. After all, one panicky soldier can affect a whole troop. Not just the morale, but even a military initiative can be ruined by one terrified trooper. Gideon must have expected a handful of lily-livered individuals from some of the other tribes to head for home. He would have been truly horrified to discover his fighting force had been cut from thirty-two thousand to ten thousand. Watching them leave, the old fears were starting to rise again. Would he have enough men to fight the mighty Midianites? But still God wasn't satisfied. Too many, Gideon. Too many, Lord? Surely not.

And so it was that three hundred men eventually triumphed for God and for Gideon. Even before that historic victory, God had left Gideon in no doubt that the outcome was going to be divinely inspired and controlled. He encouraged Gideon and his friend to eavesdrop on a discussion in the Midianite camp. They arrived in their hiding place just in time to hear one of the soldiers tell his friend 'I had a dream. A round loaf of barley bread came tumbling into the Midianite camp. It struck the tent with such force that the tent overturned and collapsed.' Purah and Gideon were amazed to hear the friend's response. 'This can be nothing other than the sword of Gideon, son of Joash, the Israelite. God has given the Midianites and the whole camp into his hands.' This divinely inspired dream led to divinely inspired panic in the camp and Gideon and his meagre force were able to rout the enemy with ease. It was no wonder Gideon had previously roused his sleeping soldiers with the words 'Get up! The Lord has given the Midianite camp into your hands.'

From obscurity to power and back again *(Judges 8:1–35)*

Sadly, that sense of God being totally in control of his life was soon to disappear. After the God-inspired battle, Gideon returned to his home town of Ophrah. Once there he made a spectacular priestly vestment known as an ephod. Each man gratefully gave Gideon an ear-ring from his plunder. From their gifts he adorned the garment so that it became breathtakingly beautiful.

Perhaps it began innocuously enough. No doubt someone, grateful for the way Gideon had cleaned the land of the Midianite scourge, bowed down in front of the ephod. It, more than anything, symbolized the glory of Gideon's achievements. As time went on, more and more bowed in front of the vestment until it became an object of worship and Israel once again prostituted themselves before an idol.

For forty years Israel knew peace from the hand of Midian and for the same number of years Gideon lived in Ophrah. We hear no more about him. The man who was rescued from obscurity by the angel of the Lord, found that once he stopped trusting in the power of God's Spirit, he discovered total obscurity. He found many wives, fathered seventy sons, watched the nation worship his home-made idol, and eventually died. And after his death, the chronicler of Judges tells his readers, he slipped completely from Israelite consciousness.

'No sooner had Gideon died than the Israelites again prostituted themselves to the Baals. They set up Baal Berith as their god and did not remember the Lord their God, who had rescued them from the hands of all their enemies on every side. They also failed to show kindness to the family of Gideon for all the good things he had done for them.'

So Gideon, the man who began life worshipping several

gods and then moved to an uncompromising faith in the one God, ended bowing down to an ephod. And, ultimately, that syncretism was what he endowed to his nation. The man who had travelled from obscurity in Ophrah to power in the valley of Harod moved back to where he had begun, symbolically and geographically.

Lessons of faith

Inferiority. Gideon's story is our story. It is easy for us to feel as helpless as he did in the face of contemporary problems. We are aware of declining church numbers, growing apathy in society towards God and enormous sociological and moral problems hitting us daily on our television screens. We are surrounded by problems every bit as intimidating as the marauding Midianites and Israel's sense of divine abandonment.

Often, like Gideon, we clutch our prized picture of ourselves and hope that God will go away and find someone else. We are far too insignificant and inferior to do anything. Like Gideon's awareness of his tribe, our background haunts us. We are working class and speak with a strong regional burr. People laugh and impersonate us whenever we join a conversation. How could God ever use us?

It is not only our birth place which can intimidate us, but also our lack of education. We fluffed our GCE's and spent a year at the tech which we also failed. Or we failed our degree and have never been able to come to terms with it. Whenever we sit in a service or read a book which challenges us to witness for God, we reach for the inferiority button. We are well programmed and the arguments start tumbling out. Besides, most of the people in our church are business men and professional women. They are far more gifted than we are. Let God use them.

Inferiority is not restricted to people who feel their background and education are in some way sub-standard. People who have risen to positions of prominence in society are often stricken by the same bug. When God challenges them to go in his strength, they bounce back with all kinds of problems. But God, I've sinned in the past and let you down. I am terribly unworthy to attempt anything so significant. Or, the argument runs, God I just don't know enough about the Bible. What happens if people ask me searching questions and I become stumped? That would be very embarrassing wouldn't it? Sorry Lord. Why don't you send that chap over there. He seems full of confidence.

And so the merry-go-round whirls around in every church: all of us thinking we are the most inadequate and inferior Christian ever to walk this earth, and everyone else thinking we are just the man or woman for the job.

Gideon reminds us that a man who saw himself as the weakest in his family and tribe was transformed into a mighty man of valour. He also reminds us that inferiority resulting from spiritual deficiency can be dealt with by a Spirit who is willing to clothe himself in us. After all, Gideon was worshipping several gods when God dealt with him. We are also reminded from his story that the feeling of intellectual inferiority which says 'I don't know enough about God', can be dealt with by a God who gradually reveals himself to his man or woman of faith. Little by little Gideon learnt the peace, power, presence and patience of God. Yet, when he started, he barely knew who God was.

Inferiority has plagued many generations of Christians. Moses felt he stammered too much to tackle Pharaoh. 'L . . . l . . . l . . . let my p . . . p . . . people go' would not exactly reduce the Egyptian despot to panic. Jeremiah believed he was too young to be a prophet and Paul considered himself the worst sinner who had ever lived.

29

Yet, all three discovered that there is a positive side to inferiority. If it becomes a reason for saying no, then it is clearly wrong. But if it leads to a position of humility where we say we can't possibly do anything, God will have to do everything, then he can transform inferiority into valour. And that's what he did for Moses, Jeremiah, Paul and Gideon. And that's what he can do for you and me. Making men and women of inferiority into men and women of faith.

Peace, power and fear. Even if we get started on our pilgrimage of faith we will inevitably encounter all kinds of difficulties. Many Christians initially manage to sidestep their inferiority and then find themselves confronted with a challenge which leaves them gibbering with fear. But they thought they were supposed to be filled with God's peace! Then one night, witnessing with friends on the streets of their home town, they are surrounded by a gang of nasty looking hell's angels, revving their anger and displaying total disregard for the things of God. So they lose their nerve and it's back to the comparative safety of the winepress and 'Please don't ask us to do anything for God again.'

Such sentiments are commonplace. They show a lack of understanding of the principle that the man of faith will have his sense of peace constantly tested. In Christian experience, peace is not given to us for palm beaches and deserted islands. It is given to us to carry us through the smell of battle and the rumblings of war. Gideon's peace was ruthlessly analysed almost immediately when he was sent to smash his father's altar. Similarly, when Jesus gave his disciples his special peace in the upper room, almost in the next breath he was telling them they must evangelize the whole world. A task which for many was to lead to persecution and death.

30

When we find our life of faith is being filled with fear, we must not think we are being inadequate Christians. Gideon's story reminds us that we are probably on the right track!

Uncertainty. The story of the fleece underlines the fact that Gideon's life of faith was riddled with uncertainty as well as fear. It had begun in that vein and seemed to continue throughout his exploits for God. At Ophrah he needed to be sure this really was God speaking to him and not just a wayfarer. Even after the outpouring of God's Spirit he needed the visible demonstration of the fleece to assure him that God was going to deliver Israel from the hands of the Midianites. Before the decisive battle in the valley of Harod, he needed the reassurance of his friend Purah as they went to listen to the Midianites expressing their fears.

Much later than Gideon, Jesus was to condemn the Jews for constantly asking for a sign. Yet God happily concedes to Gideon's request over the fleece. The riddle is resolved when we realize that for the Jews, their request was an indication of disbelief. Gideon's request was that of a young believer groping for the certainty that God is with him.

Every Christian will sometimes encounter such uncertainty. For Gideon, the doubting and uncertainty were expressed in the presence of God. He wanted to know that God was there before he attempted anything. David provides a similar model in many of his psalms. Sadly, some Christians, when faced with uncertainty, head for the security of the winepress. Away from the presence of God they fall into doubt, and become bitter and unusable in his service.

The latter years. Gideon's story ends as ignominiously as it started. An old man, he fathered many children and allowed

31

his people to worship an ephod instead of the living God. As we consider failure, one of the hallmarks of Christian failure is that as the verve and fire of youth are replaced by a secure old age, so faith begins to wane. Gideon who had rallied thirty-two thousand men for God, had lain on his belly as a spy, had clambered down a mountainside with torches and jars, ended his life spending forty years of inactivity in the obscurity of his own house. He had the warmth of the love of his own family. He also had the encouragement of the fact that the people of Israel unsuccessfully asked him to be their king. He had many stories to tell his grandchildren and many happy reflections to fill his twilight years. Yet the verve and reliance on God had gone. He played out his years to the accompaniment of a nation worshipping his ephod. He died and was soon forgotten.

Failure often accompanies Christians when the spiritual reliance of youth is replaced by the comfort of old age. If the Christian life is a pilgrimage, then old age should be full of new Christian adventures rather than distant memories. Gideon's quiet, peaceful end reminds us of the dangers of a faith which can slip ever so gently into failure.

Faith . . . but

We have seen a man who allowed the Spirit of God to use him against the backcloth of his own inadequacy. The story told in Judges lurches from triumph to defeat, back to triumph then on to defeat in an ever moving circle. His inferiority and proneness to compromise with surrounding religions, although with him all his life, were purified to such an extent that he finds his way into the Hebrews' catalogue of faith. His inferiority challenges us to consider whether *our* sense of inferiority prevents us from living and working for God. Our next hero will force us to question whether we allow our natural hesitancy to lead us to total failure or to a failure which is refined by the presence of God. And so to our next hero. Bring on Barak!

CHAPTER THREE

BARAK THE HESITANT

(JUDGES 4–5)

God said 'Go!' . . . Barak said 'No!' *(Judges 4:1–9)*

Barak would have preferred messages wrapped in vagaries.
'We were wondering in the circumstances, taking into
account your own undoubted abilities, whether you would
consider helping us some time in the future.' That type
of message was fine. It left plenty of room for uncertainty
and time for several rethinks. He could stall and ask for
a 'not inconsiderable period of time in which to consider
the gracious invitation'.

Deborah's message was almost crass. The tiny word
haunted him. 'Go!' No room for evaluation or inter-
pretation. It was terribly stark and demanding. But even
more disconcerting were the claims she made. It would be
quite easy to sidestep the overtures of Deborah. Even a
woman as dynamic and powerful as she could eventually
be subdued. But God. That was a different matter. 'The
Lord, the God of Israel commands you: Go!' Those had

been her exact words. Barak could perhaps try a certain amount of psychoanalysis. Was she sure she hadn't been overworking. After all it did get terribly hot near that tree where she held her sessions. Perhaps she had been in the sun too long. How could she be certain God had spoken?

Such an approach would have no impact on Deborah. She was convinced that God was calling Barak to lead the people of Israel against Jabin and Sisera, the leaders of the Canaanites. They had intimidated her people for twenty years. Victory was now in sight. God had told her he would give the Canaanites into the hands of Barak and his troops.

Barak could not share her certainty. As far as he was concerned, he was an unknown person in Israel. Certainly he was somebody in his own tribe of Naphtali, but this was a task for the united strength of Israel. Who was he to bring together all the disparate strands of God's nation?

Besides, he was a little concerned about the spiritual aspect. It was all very well Deborah saying God had revealed the plan to her. Why then had Barak heard nothing? Most of his heroes of the faith, like Abraham, Jacob and Moses had all experienced direct calls from God. But he only had the certainty of Deborah.

He was a fighter, not a leader of the people or a spiritual motivator. The more he thought, the more he saw Deborah in that role. She had become a judge of national repute. In the early days she had only counselled people from the Ramah and Bethel districts. As time passed, she had found herself building up a reputation for her wisdom. She was now a national figure; people came to her from all over Israel. In addition to her being a first class judge, she was also considered something of a prophetess. She often called people back to God's decrees and challenged them about their moral behaviour. She was renowned for her ability to see the future from God's perspective.

Barak was aware of her reticence. She had shared with him her own insecurity about Israel's reactions to her. The Israelites had gradually grown to accept and respect her as a judge and a prophetess. But a warrior leader? That was different. That would surely raise the traditional hackles. Fighting was for men. Surely the people would expect men to populate the battlefield and Deborah to stay under the tree.

Although he could guess her response, he braced himself and shared his compromise solution. 'If you go with me, I will go, but if you don't go with me, I won't go.'

Surprisingly, Deborah's answer was in the affirmative, although it had something of a sting in the tail.

'Very well, I will go with you,' she said. Then she added the rider which was to haunt him for the rest of his life. 'But because of the way you are going about this, the honour will not be yours, for the Lord will hand Sisera over to a woman.'

That prediction has been fulfilled down to this day. The song written to celebrate their joint victory over Sisera, is called Deborah's song by the commentators and most Bibles preface it with a similar title. This in spite of the fact that the actual Bible text informs us that Deborah and Barak wrote and sang the song.

It is so easy to expect people of faith to be those of iron resolve. People who boldly go where others fear to tread. A welter of Christian publications can give the impression that people God uses in the twentieth century are those who give an unparalleled display of certainty in everything they attempt. Such people have most of 'D' missing in their dictionaries. Doubt, despair, difficulty, despondency, depression are not there. Their books are writ large with entries under 'S'. Success, superlative, spectacular, supernatural, superior, stunning are words which fill the letters sent to prayer partners at home. They are people who expect success, and rally the troops in halls stuffed (back to 'S') with people. They tell them to go back and succeed for God.

Barak is out of place in such company. He cuts a pathetic figure insisting Deborah holds his hand in God's enterprise. Whilst he is out of place amongst some modern Christians, he has many partners in the Bible.

When God told Jonah to go, he also replied 'No.' Unlike Barak, there was not even an 'unless' clause in his response. He sailed twelve-hundred miles in the opposite direction from Nineveh, in the hope of losing God's voice somewhere on the ocean. Ananias had similar misgivings about his command to visit the murderer Paul, who, according to God, was the new hope for evangelizing the Gentiles. Moses was equally afraid of his planned visit to Pharaoh. He managed to go one better than Barak and ended up with a support group of Aaron and Miriam. Barak's story reminds us of the human failings of people of faith, but also underlines the gracious nature of our longsuffering God. Despite the fact that through history he had to share his glory with a woman, God still allowed Deborah to accompany Barak and used her to help him grow in his faith.

A tale of two faiths (*Judges 4:10–24*)

Sisera and Jabin must have often shared a little joke together. They found it a wonderful irony that not very long ago Joshua of Israel had crushed a Canaanite king with the same name. Now Jabin Mark II was greatly feared throughout Canaan and Israel. He had enjoyed the upper-hand for twenty years. He was confident that the latest uprising could easily be crushed. In fact, he could remain in Hazor. This was a job for Sisera.

Sisera was renowned for his cruelty. He believed in his own physical prowess. It came in handy in the hill country of Israel. But of course, he was especially proud of the large fleet of iron chariots he had at his disposal. They now numbered nine hundred, offering the niftiest form of transport in the east. One man stood and controlled the horses, whilst the other fired shots from his bow. Sisera allowed himself a smirk as he contemplated the battle against this unknown Barak. He and his men were gathering on the slopes of Mount Tabor. It was Sisera's hope that they would pour down the hills into the valley where he and his men would be positioned. The Israelites would be sitting-targets for his mobile marksmen. It would be embarrassing, but, mercifully, it would soon be over.

Sisera's faith in iron was short lived. The song of Barak and Deborah suggests that a sudden rainstorm grounded his force. He had to abandon his chariot and foot it to the country of the Kenites. Convinced he would be safe, he entered the tent of Jael. Exhausted by the last few days he soon fell asleep and, as he slept, the man of iron was slain by an iron tent peg.

Barak's faith was far less defined. He had been told that God would lure Sisera and his troops into the Kishon valley and give them into his hands. It all sounded grand and final at the Palm of Deborah. Up on Mount Tabor it seemed very different. He had rallied over ten thousand men, yet his forces could so easily be wiped out by those feared chariots. God had given Deborah a message for the hesitant hero. It simply said 'Go! This is the day the Lord has given Sisera into your hands. Has not the Lord gone ahead of you?' That last statement must have pleased Barak at first. Yet up on the mountain, looking down on the Canaanites it began to unsettle him. The trouble with God

38

going on before, is that you can't see him. Where has he gone? What is he going to do?

Such questions have troubled countless generations of people of faith since Barak. We often read the story of faith too quickly. We forget that between the promise of God and the enactment of the promise there is a pause. The pause is often long and agonizing. It was so for Jairus who, after asking Jesus for help for his sick daughter, was subjected to the interruption of a lady with an issue of blood. Did Jesus really have to find out who had touched him? In all the delay, the news came from the house that his daughter had died. Yet Jesus was adamant there was no need to be afraid.

The Jairus factor must have operated for Barak. He had the promise, but no clue as to how it was to be fulfilled. And in that interval of panic, his faith was shaped. Sisera had endured no such fears. His faith was placed entirely in iron machines which were overwhelmed by the Israelites and grounded by a timely deluge of rain. Sisera and his faith perished along with the faith of a mother waiting in vain for her triumphant son. Peering through the window, she decided his chariots were delayed because of the victorious plundering. No doubt he was choosing himself a sumptuous Israelite female slave. Little did she realize his faith and hers lay smashed in a Kenite tent.

It is people with no spiritual faith who map out the future and decide how things are going to be. Like Sisera, they place their faith in things which others do not possess. Sadly, the Christian church can often chide spiritual people for not defining their vision in graphic detail. It is a sign of true faith, not weakness, to follow a God who leads yet does not spell out every aspect of the future. The simple watchword 'The Lord has gone before' does not answer enough questions for many of our contemporary Christians.

So often church leaders spell out their vision to the church. Sisera's vision was in iron chariots, theirs are cast-iron theological frameworks. Like chariots they come in all shapes and sizes. There are chariots that fly through the air with charismatic ease. Chariots with no wheels, just bolstered sides, built up with solid truth. You can't see over the sides, nor can you move forward, but you feel secure. No-one can attack you. There are chariots that go as long as you have the right sort of manual. The purveyors of all these spiritual chariots are unhappy with the faith of Barak. It sounds so flimsy and almost hesitant. Yet that is the faith the church must rediscover. A faith that does not know what God will do, or how he will do it, but believes that he will act mightily. Such was the faith of Barak the hesitant, who, believing that the Lord had gone ahead, followed . . . eventually.

Risky faith

God rarely makes faith easy. The startled Barak was told to face the legendary might of Sisera and his iron chariots. Looking back on his escapade he was convinced that he and his people of Naphtali had risked their lives for God and Israel.

The common view of the life of faith, restricted to coffee-elongated meetings in centrally-heated churches, is blown apart by Barak and his men. Similarly, Jesus offered his followers a life of risk. The partners of Zebedee and Son Fishing Company were told to leave their secure business and follow Jesus. James and John were later told that they would have to suffer in a similar way to Jesus. Those who were married, such as Peter, were told that they would have nowhere to lay their heads. All the disciples were told that the model for their Christian pilgrimage was a cross with all its stigma and cruelty. Unlike the modern church, the disciples would not spiritualize the concept. They knew that to follow a carpenter, who claimed to be God, rendered them liable to the death sentence for blasphemy.

The Jesus of the Bible has not changed, nor has his challenge. He still calls us to a radical life of risk. A life where we risk rejection of friends and family when they see that 'Jesus is Lord' is a basis for living and not just a line from a rousing chorus. It is a life where we often risk losing our security or the realization of a life-long ambition. To soften the blow we have made faith cerebral. We have compressed it into a package of facts rather than an ongoing dynamic experience which brings us into conflict with the purveyors of traditional religion and material security. Christians who live such a life of risk find it difficult. So did Barak. The difficulty arises when the rest of God's people find the challenges of the risky man of faith unpalatable.

Naphtali and Zebulun risked their lives with Barak. But others were not quite so sure. Dan stayed by their ships and Asher remained on the sea coast near their coves. The Reubenites were not so immediately dismissive in their response. Sitting near their fires they had a long period of heart-searching. The chief elder no doubt urged his flock to consider carefully whether they should follow this little-known brother Barak. So they searched their hearts and said 'No!' Perhaps they spiritualized their response. They weren't sure that Israel was ready just yet. Was it really God's timing? After all, the threat had been there for twenty years. Why all this frenetic talk about defeating the enemy now? Surely it would be better to sit by the fire and grow spiritually; to enjoy the love of God and study his Word more fully before they went to confront the foe. Anyway, if they were to go, they must get to know each other better.

41

They were going to be thrown together on those heights in all kinds of weather. They would have to share basic camping facilities. Such a venture would never work unless their friendship deepened. They must concentrate on fellowship before this dangerous outreach. So they threw another log on the fire and sang another tear-jerking verse of their favourite Hebrew chorus.

And Barak the hesitant, who had eventually gone for God, learnt that God's people couldn't cope with a risky man of faith. Of course, they didn't call their hesitancy cowardice. They had a far better phrase. They probably wrote a memo to Barak and assured him that after much heart-searching they were spiritually uncertain whether this venture was God's will.

Barak and Deborah sing their song *(Judges 5:1–31)*

Despite Barak's disappointment that Reuben, Dan and Asher failed to join the cause, we find that his story ends with him in exultant form. Barak the hesitant became the hallelujah man. His faith erupted into the song which he and Deborah composed and sang.

The man who wanted to withdraw from the presence of a God who told him to go, now wanted to praise him.

'I will sing to the Lord, I will sing.
I will make music to the Lord, the God of Israel.'

They were not deep or penetrating sentiments but were from the heart. So much so, his song was full of commands to the people. 'Hear this, you kings,' he sang, 'listen to this, you rulers.' He even directed imperatives towards Deborah and himself.

'Wake up, wake up, Deborah!
Wake up, wake up, break out in song!
Arise, O Barak!
Take captive your captives, O son of Abinoam.'

This is no solo or duet. It's a song for all the people. The princes, the rulers, the women drawing their water, Jael and the Kenites, in fact, everybody who loves the Lord. All are invited to take the floor and join Barak for a song of joy.

The spontaneous response to God is a hallmark of many people of faith in the Old Testament. Moses and Miriam also led the people in a song and dance after the momentous victory against Pharaoh and the Egyptians. As faith evolves, through doubts, questions and mistakes, it should always arrive at a point where it wants to leap for joy and thank God. At that point of realization that life had been risked, that God had calmed his fears and routed the enemy, Barak wanted to thank him from the bottom of his heart. Perhaps it is this type of faith that can respond best in such a spontaneous way. The person who, knowing he should go for God, holds back, then reluctantly goes, is the person who, when the promises of God are fulfilled, will rejoice in the goodness and patience of a God who perseveres with a hesitant follower.

Barak's song, for all its spontaneity and joy, did not lack solid content. He had reflected long and hard on what God had done and the song reflected his thinking.

Faith for fear

Barak was amazed when he began to consider the change God had brought about in Israel. For eighteen years the nation had been paralysed by the Canaanite threat. Even the existence of forty thousand trained fighters had not been able to rouse national fervour. People had lived in so much fear that village-life had ceased as people remained in their homes, afraid of attacks from armies of marauding foreigners.

But now it was different. People at the watering places recited what God had done. Popular songs were composed and sung, so that people who had once drawn their water furtively and quickly, now lingered to talk about the marvellous transformation in Israel. In his song, Barak encourages travellers to slow down and listen to the revellers.

The faith of one man can often lead to the transformation of a whole community. Jonah, a prophet who was even more reluctant than Barak, saw the cruel city of Nineveh changed by his preaching of judgment. One hundred and twenty thousand people were suddenly transformed from lovers of pagan militaristic strength, to worshippers of God. According to Mark, many of the physcially and mentally sick of Capernaum were brought to Jesus one evening. The brief statement that Jesus healed them, hides the magnitude of the change that must have taken place in that community. Synagogue approach roads which had been crammed with beggars, were now empty as the healed took their place again in society. Just as Barak's faith was rewarded by his community being changed, so modern people of faith should expect their mighty God to act in towns, villages and cities. Often we restrict God to church and think that the problems of twentieth-century Britain are too complex for him to solve. We should be following a God whom we expect to work. The laughter and chatter at the watering holes is ample testimony to the fact that modern faith as fragile as Barak's could be rewarded in such a way. Supermarkets, garages and restaurants would then be filled with people telling each other what God has done in their community.

The Barak blockage

If Gideon's inferiority prevents some people from becoming active men and women of faith, then many more suffer from Barak's hesitancy. When God tells us to go, it somehow seems more natural to say 'No.' Very rarely is our response as bald as that. Normally we can do much better, by unearthing all kinds of hidden factors of which we're quite sure God wasn't aware.

A young couple have just moved in to number two. At first the girl seems slightly lost. She has two young children and is alone most of the day. Her husband leaves early in the morning and returns about six at night. You see her walking around the estate with the two infants and feel an inner voice telling you to talk to her and invite her for coffee. But Lord, you counter, I would but you know I've got my own chores. As she doesn't know anyone she might become too dependent and come in to my house every day. What happens if I can't get rid of her? I'll leave it a while, until she's more established. Besides, Lord, her children are tiny and mine are teenageers. I've lost the art of nappy talk. I really wouldn't know what to say.

As the weeks roll into months, the Jehovah Witnesses call on you. You give them short shrift and they call at number two. It is not long before Roger and Gill are peddling copies of *The Watchtower* around the estate and attending all their meetings. You kick yourself and mutter something about if only you'd realized they were looking for something spiritual you'd have been there as quick as lightning. But it's too late; the Barak blockage has taken its toll.

It is not just on modern estates that this principle seems to be at work. In universities and colleges hordes of bemused freshers enter the academic gates looking for friendship and support. At the same time, many students from abroad register for courses of study. In these first days they are often open to friendship and the gospel. As time passes, individuals within both groups find their own circle of friends and become hardened to any advance from someone trying to penetrate the circle.

Although hesitancy can cripple Christian witness, it is clear from Barak's story it can be cured. For him, he had to accept that God was going before him. The sight of Sisera and his chariots made him tremble with caution but God stressed to him and to Deborah that they must trust him to go ahead of them. It is this aspect of faith we all find difficult. If we knew exactly what God was going to do, with several assurances that everything was going to turn out all right, then perhaps our faith would be a little more active. As it is, he takes us to the top of the hill and tells us to enter into the valley of battle and not to panic. Or he takes us to the front door of Roger and Gill's house and, as our knees knock in time to our gurgling stomachs, he tells us to go in his strength. Yet remarkably we always find that where we have committed the project to God in prayer, he does go before us.

Of course, for Barak there was an added dimension to his movement from hesitancy to faith. As a child of Israel, he would have learnt from infancy how God promised to lead his people. Such a promise for the future was always against the backcloth of a fulfilled promise in the past. When Moses was encouraging his kinsmen to believe that God would deliver them from Egypt, he was making his speeches to a nation which was now so large, the Pharaoh was frightened of its militaristic potential. This very fact was a fulfilment of the promise God had made to Abraham, that his descendants would one day be as numerous as the stars of the sky. So Moses was in effect saying, God tells us he will help us and if you wonder how we can be certain of his promise, just remember how he has performed in the past.

It was the same for Gideon and Barak. As God predicted deliverance from Midianites and Canaanites, they could both look back to the momentous act of God in the exodus of his people from bondage.

And so it can be for men and women of faith today. The God who meets us and promises his presence has fulfilled so many more predictions than he had for Barak. He has honoured his statements made eight centuries earlier and sent Jesus to die for our sins and raised him from the dead. Such a God will not let us down on the estate or college campus. When he promises to go ahead of us and we hesitate, he encourages us to look back on history and see the way in which he has gone ahead of his people.

Such faith will fashion us into men and women who can be used by God. Our hesitancy will probably always be there clashing with the certainties of God. But, like Barak, we must offer it up to God so that when he tells us to go, we go, even if it is eventually rather than immediately.

So, inferiority and hesitancy can be used by a faithful God. In some ways they are emotions which lend themselves to divine assurance. If we suffer from them we must never feel God can't use us. But what about the other side of the coin? The Christian who is very 'showy' and outrageous? Unlike Gideon and Barak he never suffers from nerves for a second. Rumbles in stomachs are felt by people around him rather than himself. He is prepared to take

47

anything and anyone on. In fact, you sometimes feel he is massaging his own ego rather than serving God. What about him? Can God use him? Well, yes. I think it's time we met . . . Mr Samson.

CHAPTER FOUR

SAMSON THE FLIPPANT

(JUDGES 13–16)

The parent's plea *(Judges 13:1–25)*

He had never been so frightened in all his life.

For the past few days his wife had filled him with news of a divine visitor. Frankly he had been uncertain what to think. For many years they had wanted a child, yet for some reason his wife had remained barren. Now there were tales of messengers from heaven saying she was going to produce a boy. No ordinary boy. A special one who was to lead the beleaguered forces of Israel, and take the Nazirite vow.

Manoah had worried about his wife's news. Perhaps the pressure was finally getting to her. Her own emotional strain and that caused by the young women of Zorah parading their offspring through the village was finally telling. He had done what he felt was best. During evening devotions he asked God to send the visitor again so that they could clarify one or two matters. Of course, he disguised his mild doubts about the episode.

Now he shivered with fear. Sure enough the messenger had returned and confirmed his wife's story. Only now was he beginning to think through the implications. Manoah, a humble man of Zorah, had looked into his face. He had actually talked with God. It was now his turn to be startled. 'Surely,' he said, 'I shall die.' For Manoah knew that all the great men of God had been afraid to look at God.

It was his wife's turn to reassure him, pointing out that if God had wished to kill them, he would not have accepted their burnt offering nor returned a second time. Manoah was consoled and he and his wife pieced together the angel's news.

They were to receive a boy who was to be different from all others. He was to be subject to the Nazirite vow, not just from birth but from conception. His mother was not to imbibe any strong drink; nor was he. Manoah knew from his education that as a Nazirite his son would not be allowed to touch the carcass of a dead animal or human. The divine guest had also underlined that his hair must never be cut. This would be the visual sign that he was God's man.

So Manoah and his wife waited with expectation. Finally, their son was born and they called him Samson. No-one gurgling over the crib asked why they'd chosen the name. They knew the story behind Samson. And as the exultant parents nursed their child, the onlookers knew how Manoah believed he would fulfil the expectations of his name 'radiant as the sun'. The old man had told them all how Israel's sun had gone down. The light of the Philistines overwhelmed the Jews with fear. Talk of Jehovah was muted and rare. But Manoah's child was going to change all that. God's sun was going to come up again and he was thrilled to be a small part of the new day.

Pilgrim's regress

Manoah and his wife made sure that Samson heard the story of the angel. Many times he was reminded of the three-fold nature of the Nazirite vow. As he grew up, the boy stood out from the others. His plaited locks of hair were a talking point amongst the children and parents. He knew from his father that this was the cue for him to explain his unusual origins and the hopes of his parents.

Despite the heady days of life before Samson's conception and birth, it didn't take long for the pious father to see that his son was not totally what he'd expected. The radiant sun began to wane. Manoah saw a strong self-will move through childhood into a difficult adolescence. Samson was very much his own man.

During his teenage years, he often walked in to the neighbouring Philistine towns. At first he went with friends, then increasingly alone. Manoah was unsure how to react. He was very keen that his son should see the superiority of the Israelite way of life. He wanted him to grow up unstained by the superstition and religious pluralism of the Philistines. He also wanted him to grow up into a defender of the ways of God. Surely this was best done by staying away from pagan influence. Yet at the same time, he was to do a special work for the Israelites against the Philistines. This being so, perhaps it was as well for him to acquaint himself with the Philistine way of life. It was this acquaintance which was to lead to his downfall.

I want that woman *(Judges 14:1-11)*

After another sortie into Philistine territory, Samson returned home in a determined mood. He was fairly certain how his parents would react, yet he had to tell them. So

51

he blurted it out. He had been down to Timnah and seen the most beautiful woman you could imagine. Samson's youthful eyes lit up as he recalled her stunning looks.

His father's reaction was fairly predictable. Quoting the law of Moses, he reminded Samson that God was not keen on marriages between his people and pagan nations. Manoah had anticipated this moment for many months. It had filled him with dread. He recited the whole passage as he warned his son of the dangers of the woman of Timnah.

'Be careful not to make a treaty with those who live in the land; for when they prostitute themselves to their gods and sacrifice to them, they will invite you and you will eat their sacrifices. And when you choose some of their daughters as wives for your sons and those daughters prostitute themselves to their gods, they will lead your sons to do the same.'

Samson was as adamant as his father. Yes, he knew God's law. No, he didn't want to displease God. Yes, this was true love. No, he didn't really want to disobey his parents. Yes, of course he would still see them. No, he hadn't forgotten his Nazirite vow. Yes, he realized the great sacrifices his parents had made for him. No, he didn't agree this action was destroying all their hopes and prayers. Anyway, perhaps God would be in the marriage somehow.

The chronicler of Judges takes up this point and informs us that his 'parents did not know that this was from the Lord who was seeking an occasion to confront the Philistines'. We are left wondering whether Samson knew the deeper purpose of God or whether he merely reacted to his own sensuous feelings. Whatever his understanding, God was at work in the situation at Timnah. Yet as the story unfolds, we see alongside God's blessing, the human failing of Samson.

Whilst his parents reluctantly negotiated the wedding, the Spirit of the Lord fell upon him. In that divine strength he slayed a lion, something which, as a Nazirite, he should not have done because of the necessity of touching the carcass of the dead animal. Realizing what he had done, he concealed news of the feat from his parents.

Much later, when he returned to Timnah to claim his bride, he found that bees had made a hive in the carcass. He took honey home for his parents but still could not bring himself to tell them where it came from. He had had too much confrontation with them already and didn't want another argument.

So God's laws were falling like skittles. Marrying a pagan woman, touching the carcass of a dead animal and failing to obey his father and mother. Of course, there was more to follow. No-one reading the narrative of the wedding feast at Timnah raging for seven days can imagine Samson sitting in the lounge clutching a Band of Hope abstention-certificate. The events which led to the riddle, the slaughter of thirty men and the loss of his wife all seem to owe more to the spirit of alcohol than the Spirit of the Lord.

Blessing and failure are two strange bedfellows appearing time and again in Samson's life. The marriage, which should have been filled with God's blessing, was peopled by his wife's relatives and not his own. It was in her home because Samson's family were opposed to the match. Instead of a relaxed atmosphere with friends and well-wishers, the seven-day festivities were watched over by thirty bodyguards – a group of men given to Samson by a father-in-law who anticipated the danger of having a ruler of Israel as a son-in-law. 'What if some of the Philistines try to lynch him during the ceremony,' he had reasoned. And so a time of rejoicing was filled with tension.

The exhibition of strength which could have encouraged

the dispirited Jews to see that God was in control and would deliver them through Samson, was seen by no-one except the lion. Even his parents, who could have spread news to their kinsfolk, were not told because he used God's strength on an enterprise which broke one of his vows and because he was growing more and more isolated from them. Indeed, the isolation was so great that after the wedding at Timnah, Manoah and his wife are rarely mentioned again.

Yet, through all this, God was somehow at work. In a land where people did what was right in their own eyes, Jehovah, the Lord, was still breaking through. Despite Samson's own impetuous nature, God was still deeply involved in the story.

A riddle and a rout *(Judges 14:12–20)*

On the first day of the feast, Samson threw out a challenge to his bodyguards. The riddle was given to them 'Out of the eater, something to eat; out of the strong something sweet.' Confident that no-one knew anything about his exploits with the lion, he offered the reward of thirty linen garments and thirty changes of clothes to be distributed among them if they deciphered the riddle within the seven days of the feast. Samson clearly underestimated the depth of his challenge. They were not prepared to be beaten by this foreigner. They mused over the puzzle but at the end of the fourth day were nowhere near a solution. In desperation they turned to Samson's wife. Thirty brawny bodyguards threatening to burn her house, herself and her family unless she co-operates, gained the desired effect. For three days she turned in a performance worthy of Hollywood's Bette Davis; throwing herself at her husband in uncontrollable bouts of sobbing. Samson finally broke and revealed the secret, which in turn was conveyed to the exultant bodyguards.

When Samson was humiliated on the final day of the feast, he left Timnah and headed for Ashkelon. There, under the influence of the power of God, he slayed thirty men and gave their clothes to the winners of the wager. Raging with anger, he deserted his wife and returned to his father's home.

Vengeance is sweet *(Judges 15:1-9)*

Things are always different the day after an argument. In the heat of the moment at Timnah, Samson had felt justified in storming out and heading back home. How could his wife have betrayed him? He also felt vindicated by the events of Ashkelon. After all, the bodyguards had plotted together to try and disgrace him. So what was wrong with slaying thirty people to acquire the garments to pay the wager?

Then as the days wore on he saw that face again. The same look which had reduced him to jelly. The face that had made him go against the wishes of his godly parents and endure a terrible atmosphere in the home. The more he tried to think of other things, the more the face appeared. And the more he saw the face, the more he knew he loved her. He wanted her so badly he resolved to return to Timnah.

His parents had been loving and accepting over the past traumatic weeks. They had been thrilled to have him back around the farm. Now as he went to get a young goat to take as a peace offering, he knew he would have a lot of explaining to do. Yet he knew that he had to go. His emotions demanded it, so he set out on the road for Timnah.

The instant Samson's father-in-law saw him approach the house he panicked. It was time for quick thinking. Making sure his daughter didn't see him, he rushed out. Barring the way, he told Samson as politely and firmly as possible that as far as he was concerned the marriage was dead. After all, he had left them high and dry after the wedding. His daughter was so upset she had married the best man. One glance at Samson's face told him that the conversation was not going as he'd hoped. In desperation he offered Samson his other daughter. 'She's prettier and younger than your wife. Why don't you settle for her?' he asked.

Samson's chilling response to this offer rings through the rest of his story. 'This time I have a right to get even with the Philistines; I will really harm them.' From now on Samson embarked on an orgy of violence. The thirty foxes tied together to become living torches wreaked havoc in the Philistine wheat fields. In retaliation, the Philistines destroyed his wife, his father-in-law and the rest of the family. This elicited Samson's response 'Since you've acted like this, I won't stop until I get my revenge on you.' Single-handed he went down into the town and slaughtered many of the Philistines. This lead to the Philistines grouping as a military force and entering the territory of Judah. Reasoning that he had handled thirty men comfortably but an army was a different matter, Samson escaped into the hill country and hid in a cave in the rock of Etam.

It was in that cave Samson displayed his own failure. Completely alone, unable to return to his family or the Philistine people whose friendship he briefly courted, he must have had time to reflect on his situation.

From then on there are very few references to the Spirit of God falling upon him. He was consumed by his own desire for vengeance. As his story unfolds we see more and more of Samson and less and less of God.

The Etam exile *(Judges 15:10–13)*

We are not told how many days Samson spent in the cave alone. Nor are we told how he spent his time. We do not know whether he felt remorse for the way things had turned out. We are told, however, that he was approached by a delegation representing three thousand men of Israel.

They were frightened by the advance of the outraged Philistines. Afraid that they may never own Judah, they approached Samson in the cave.

Their message was brief and simple. As far as they were concerned, the Philistines were their overlords and they had no inclination to change. Samson was in danger of ruining the uneasy peace. They had come to bind him and hand him over.

Remarkably, Samson agreed, on the condition that they would not kill him, but pass him on to the Philistines.

So, Samson the leader of Israel was betrayed by the people he had been called to lead. This betrayal is a symbol of the way in which he had become isolated from his people. Whereas Gideon had sent out the call to many of the tribes to go out in the strength of God, Samson had never managed such unity. Even if he had seen his mission in these terms, he had failed to spread the vision. Instead, the God-given power had been used selfishly to satisfy his own greed for vengeance. Now the people saw him as a threat rather than as a potential deliverer.

A slot-machine God *(Judges 15:14–19)*

Despite his isolation from the Israelites and God he still managed the odd prayer. One such was after his victory over the Philistines when the Israelites attempted to hand him over. Filled with God's power he broke free from the

57

new ropes tied securely around his hands. Then brandishing the jaw bone of an ass he slayed the hated enemy.

After the excitement of the victory and after the confused Israelites and demoralized Philistines had fled, Samson was left alone. In his solitude he began to feel the heat. The stultifying atmosphere made him thirsty. He could not find water and did not know of a nearby stream. His thirst grew so that he felt he would soon die.

In his total despair, he muttered his prayer: 'You have given your servant this great victory. Must I now die of thirst and fall into the hands of the uncircumcised?'

It is a remarkable prayer in that we are no longer used to Samson responding in a spiritual way. He had regressed from the man set aside for God, to a person who had broken two of his three Nazirite vows and many other laws of God. We are used to Samson living for himself, getting out of tight corners with his own initiative. We are also used to him following his own sensuous passions in his relationships with women and his desire for vengeance. Now this tough man was prepared to pray. Like the tough guy in the hospital bed who, faced with the prospect of cancer, will cry 'God help me', Samson turned to his God in a crisis.

Yet the prayer is not really a credit to Samson. His mention of the victory was little more than a lead in to his own problem. There was no dwelling on the victory of God, like Moses and Barak had done before him. His lack of appreciation for the help of God is shown in the name he gave to the place of victory. He called it Ramath Lehi – jaw-bone hill. The victory was the donkey's rather than God's. There was no bestowing a name rich with symbolism, so that future generations could tread the hill and remind each other that this was where God delivered Samson. As far as he was concerned, this was the place where he had triumphed with just a little help from part

of a donkey's anatomy. His song celebrated his version of
the incident:

> 'With a donkey's jaw bone
> I have made donkeys of them
> With a donkey's jaw bone
> I have killed a thousand men.'

In his prayer, he tried to buy God off with a brief mention
of the fact that God had given him a great victory. Then
in a hurt voice he cried 'Must I now die of thirst?'

God was the divine 'slot-machine'. Samson had turned
the handle and struck the jackpot of a thousand dead
Philistines. Now he wrenched the handle again. This time
he wanted to strike water. It is a prayer that has a terrible
modern ring. It is the prayer of the man who demands that
God sorts out his financial mess or gets him through his
degree examinations. It is basically the prayer of a man
who has lost a daily communion with God. It is also the
prayer of someone who has suddenly enjoyed God's blessing
after a long estrangement from him. Instead of the
experience humbling him and bringing a state of
repentance, Samson had become blasé and expected God
to answer his every wish.

Slot-machine prayers inevitably carry a justification
clause. The justification clause always sounds pious and
spiritual. So it is with Samson's prayer. He reasoned that
if he didn't find water soon he would die. That would mean
he would be taken by the Philistines. So he fed the
justification chit in to his divine machine. 'Must I now die
of thirst and fall into the hands of the uncircumcised!' It
sounds so spiritual. Taken at face value here is a man crying
to God and asking him to keep him unstained from the
sin of uncircumcised people. The spirituality soon

evaporates when we realize that a fear of linking himself with the uncircumcised Philistines never concerned Samson. He was more than happy to be contaminated by the woman of Timnah, the prostitute of Gaza and Delilah.

Even more remarkable than Samson's prayer is the fact that God answers his request. Samson drank the water and was strong enough to move on to his next major disaster.

O my! Delilah! *(Judges 16:1–19)*

Hollywood movies always depict romantic stories as fast moving and exhilarating. They move from the 'not sure' to the 'passionately committed' within two hours. They slot neatly between the adverts and when the credits come up, the two lovers sink into the celluloid horizon with Mantovani music serenading them into their cloudless future. In one hundred and twenty minutes everything is resolved and the future looks healthy.

Real romances never quite work like that. Samson tried in Gaza to slot his relationship with the prostitute into the allotted time. Sadly for him, he was detected as he stalked into the city. Realizing the men of the city were lying in wait for him he managed to rip the gates off the posts and break free undetected.

He had not enjoyed such an easy escape from the clutches of the woman of Timnah. That episode had dominated his life for far too long. The rejections by his own people had emanated from that one ill-advised relationship. David the king was later to find a similar principle at work, when his one night stand with Bathsheba led to revolt within his family and in his kingdom.

The problems caused by the women of Timnah and Gaza seem minute in comparison with the problems caused by Delilah!

In the warm summer evenings of Sorek the two lovers were sharing their childhood secrets. Like many lovers before and after them, they wanted to know everything about each other before they met. Their backgrounds were so different they enjoyed telling each other about their Philistine and Jewish upbringings. One thing bothered Delilah. 'Why,' she asked, 'are you so strong?' Brought up on the superstition of Philistine cults she believed there had to be some cultic explanation for her new friend's superhuman strength. Samson was not aware that she had ulterior motives. The men of Sorek had offered her vast sums of money if she discovered how they could overpower him.

Samson was anxious to have no secrets from his new love. After all, this was the real thing. Timnah and Gaza were just passing phases. He was mature and knew that his love for Delilah was deep and genuine. So why not tell her?

Samson still had a modicum of spiritual understanding. He knew that he was strong because God had endowed him with the power of his spirit. His long hair, never cut throughout his life, was a symbol that he was God's man. If ever that was to be touched, more than his hair would be cut. His relationship with God would also be finished. He would have destroyed the final part of his vow to God. It was only this obedience which tenuously held Samson in a relationship with his God.

So, on different occasions when Delilah persisted in trying to discover his strength, he tried to throw her off the scent by offering her wrong information. Wet ropes and new dry ropes are all applied with no effect. The Philistines, secretly hidden, were disappointed twice. On the third occasion Samson was obviously weakening. He almost gave the game away. He told her that if she wove his seven braids of hair into her loom and then pinned the

61

hair down, he would be weak. Again Delilah obeyed his instructions and when he had fallen into another drunken stupor, she went for the money. The cry 'Samson the Philistines are upon you' was as ineffective as on the other two occasions. Samson leapt up and freed himself easily, pulling the loom with him.

Delilah was now growing desperate. Three times the Philistines had been disappointed. The money may not be hers after all. Besides, the threat of burning down the house could become her experience just as it did for the woman of Timnah and her family. It was clearly time for the water-works act. For days she wept and threw herself at him. 'Don't you love me?' she asked tauntingly, again and again.

A man who had faced a lion and over a thousand Philistines without fear, found the daily nagging of Delilah too much to handle. He became so tired with it that he'd rather die than endure this constant nagging and prodding. So he gave in and told her everything.

'No razor has ever been used on my head because I have been a Nazirite, set apart to God since birth. If my head were shaved, my strength would leave me, and I would become as weak as any other man.'

It is at this point that the story of Samson is finished. God who had persisted with him through all his questionable exploits now leaves him. The final cord has been cut and Samson, as he predicted, is no different from any other man. Every man and woman of God has a secret source of strength. Although none of us has it in the measure of Samson, we all possess the Spirit of God living in us. People who do not know God, will always be trying to discover it, not so that they too can possess it, but so that they can control us. The man at the party who can say 'This is Mike who is an evangelical, Bible-believing Christian' can reduce Mike to an embarrassment and continue in the belief that he has control over him. If Mike were allowed to express himself naturally and quietly, the peace he possesses would grow and become something the guests felt was impressive and something they didn't have.

Jesus warned of the danger of casting pearls before swine. Mark the gospel writer also tells us that when people discovered who Jesus was, he often forbade them to tell anyone. The secret must be preserved and allowed to flourish and express itself in its own way; not to be controlled and bandied about by people who do not fully understand its significance.

Samson's secret was now well and truly out, and when he heard the cry 'Samson the Philistines are upon you' he found, to his horror, that his power was gone.

God takes his leave *(Judges 16:20–22)*

When Samson came round after his sleep, he thought 'I'll go out as before and shake myself free.' But he did not know that the Lord had left him. So writes the author of Judges, describing the events after his hair had been shorn.

That statement is one of the most chilling in Scripture. Samson the mighty roused himself to do as he had always done. In the past, despite his lack of spirituality, God had always helped him when he had been in a tight corner; surely God would help him now. The 'as before' principle permeates church history and the life-story of many Christians. Individual churches often press on from year to year, following the same pattern as before. God helped them in the past so he'll come to their aid again. Preachers can often mount the pulpit steps with very little spiritual preparation. They can assume that, as God has blessed their thoughts to past congregations, he will come to their aid in this service. Like Samson they expect God to bless 'as before' and forget that God may withdraw his Spirit when an individual transfers his allegiance to another power. He told unfaithful Israel that he would not always strive with them. In the same way he often withdraws his special blessing from people who have been used by him in the past. Christian fame can be a dangerous acquisition for any person who does not constantly seek God's presence.

At this point in the story Samson seems unaware that God's Spirit has been gradually withdrawing. In the beginning of his ministry he was constantly endued with God's special power. When he entered Timnah we read that the Spirit of the Lord came upon him, even though he misused that power in slaying the lion. In the same way we are told that the Spirit of the Lord came upon him when he was led captive by his own people to the Philistines. The Spirit's power enabled him to release the bonds and break free, but again he misappropriated God's power in brandishing the jaw-bone and slaying many people. Before this particular incident, the Spirit was also on him when he entered Ashkelon. Through the Spirit's power he was able to slay thirty men, take their garments and give them to the waiting bodyguards in Timnah. Apart from these incidents, the story of Samson rolls on with no further reference to the Spirit of God, except for the final incident in his life. There is no mention of the Spirit in Samson's escapade in the wheatfields where foxes became living torches and destroyed the Philistine harvest. Nor is God mentioned in the superhuman effort of wrenching the city gate off the posts at Gaza. These incidents show Samson the man anticipating that he can do everything as before, unaware of God's displeasure. In Delilah's room his assumption that God would get him out of his difficulty is misplaced. He found that all his strength had gone and the Philistines at last had their man.

Mr Samson entertains *(Judges 16:23–30)*

News travelled fast. The towns of Ashkelon and Gaza rejoiced. The rulers of the Philistines met and heard reports from the captors. Samson it seemed was now being held in Gaza.

One or two of the committee were a little concerned. What if this was nothing more than a ploy? After all, hadn't Samson been captured before, by his own people? They all knew what had happened after that.

The older men shuddered, but a bright-eyed young committee member piped up. They had no need to fear Samson. He was not even a quarter of the man he was. His strength had completely gone. His eyes had been gouged out in the prison camp and he was in bronze shackles, so there was no chance of escape. He was so harmless, that he was led around the prison compound by a young lad. Of course, they were putting Samson to good use. Although he no longer possessed the terrifying strength of before, his bulky frame meant that he came in handy grinding corn. Some of the older men smiled as they enjoyed the irony. Here was Samson, the man who once recklessly destroyed their harvest, now helping the Philistine economy by grinding corn. The bright young thing allowed himself a public titter. 'Isn't it amazing,' he said, 'to think that one night we had Samson in Gaza but he broke out and wrecked the city gates. Now he's back. I can't see him breaking out this time.'

The whole table broke out into rapturous applause and back slapping. Well done the bright young thing. Then one of the older men lopped in a slice of piety. 'Thanks be to Dagon our God.' 'Hear, hear,' the table chortled. 'I think,' said the old man, 'we should proclaim a special holiday and have celebrations outside Dagon's temple to thank him.'

The motion was carried unanimously. There was to be a huge sacrifice followed by music, entertainment and feasting. The people of all the villages, towns and cities of Philistia were to be encouraged to attend.

The young boy had never seen such crowds. He was almost hoarse with shouting. 'Let us through, let us through' he yelled at the top of his voice. Fortunately the crowd were in good humour. When they saw who he was pulling on the end of his rope they were even happier. Samson the scourge of their nation was now tottering towards the steps of their temple. A huge eyeless giant, he looked more like a beast than a man. They punched him, spat at him and jeered.

When he eventually made centre stage at the top of the steps, a huge roar went up. Then the orchestra struck up and the choir joined in. It was a catchy little number and soon the entire crowd were singing and tapping their feet.

'Our God has delivered
our enemy into our hands.
the one who laid waste our land
and multiplied our slain.'

Samson had had enough. The jeering and celebration of the people finally got to him. The joys of Delilah and his wife at Timnah seemed to be in another existence. He couldn't believe that he was in this mess. Then he thought of his mother and father and their countless warnings. Is this what they feared?

He called the boy over and asked him to place him between the central pillars and to put his hands on them. The boy complied probably thinking Samson was going to sing or tell a funny story.

Once there, Samson prayed as he'd never prayed before. The brashness of jaw-bone hill had gone. 'O God,' he said, 'remember me.' It could have been as much of a question as it was a request. 'Please strengthen me just once more.' At last Samson had got the message. It had taken him a long time, but in the prison he had had many hours to think. In those long periods of solitude he had grown to see that he could not do everything as before. He now realized that the God who was with him in his early years, left him in Delilah's room. He knew that by breaking all the Nazirite vows he had not kept his side of the bargain and God had withdrawn. Now he pleaded with God to return. The request 'let me with one blow get revenge on the Philistines for my two eyes' smacks a little of the vengeful Samson of old, but God heard his prayer and answered.

God's reason for answering his demand was far deeper than answering a call for vengeance. In fact Samson's thirst for avenging himself had been one of the reasons God had withdrawn in the first place. God was far from happy with the celebrations at Gaza that afternoon.

He had noted with sadness that, whereas at Ramoth Lehi Samson had celebrated his own strength, at least the misguided Philistines had given their praise not to themselves or their captors, but to their god. It was this which displeased him. Samson had been chosen to lead his own people and deliver them from the Philistines. Instead he had indulged himself in the gift God had given him and had become increasingly entangled with the people he was sent to act against, and increasingly isolated from the people he was sent to deliver. This afternoon should have been filled with cries of the Philistines asking the God of Israel to save them. Just like the Egyptians before them, their lips should have been full of a new name, Jehovah of Israel.

Instead the conversation was all about Dagon, and God's ambassador was a humiliated heap on the steps of Dagon's temple. It was this that prompted God to hear his prayer.

The strength came back and the temple crashed to the ground with more people slain in that afternoon than in the entire twenty-year reign of Samson the judge. The last words heard from the temple steps were huge with irony 'Let me die with the Philistines.' Samson who had courted the acceptance of two camps died in one, isolated from the other.

Funeral orations

Sermons at funerals can be taxing and demanding for the speaker. An old Welsh minister once told a funeral congregation 'Make sure that when your minister comes to bury you, he has something positive to say.' If funeral orations had been the norm in Samson's day, what, I wonder, would the minister have scribbled on his note pad? No doubt there would be several beginnings and just as many corrections. How do you adulate a man who was given so many divine gifts and yet squandered them out of his own selfish lust for power and vengeance?

Samson's family must have faced a similar problem as they made the journey from Israel to Philistia and back. Perhaps they recalled the hopes of his godly father, waxing eloquent about a sun which was going to shine for ever. As they placed Samson's corpse in Manoah's tomb, they must have wondered whether his father had died from a broken heart.

Yet, despite all these understandable frustrations about his life, the writer of Hebrews happily inserts Samson as an example of faith alongside David, Samuel and company. The supernatural strength had been given to him as a symbol of what God could do. Israel had been demoralized for many years by the incessant ravaging of their land by the Philistines. The God of heaven, who has power over storms, stars, sky and sea, encapsulated into one man a demonstration of his stunning power. The exploits against lions, foxes, hundreds of individual Philistines and the huge throng outside Dagon's temple, were intended to bring Israel to a realization that God was on their side and would protect and could ultimately deliver them. It is this positive representation of God's power which Hebrews highlights when it goes on to say that these men of faith 'shut the mouths of lions and escaped the edge of the sword'. Looking at Samson's story through Christian eyes, we begin to see that Samson the judge was a symbol or type of Christ who would come as the great deliverer from death and sin and would eventually judge not just Israel, but the whole world.

With our right emphasis on moral integrity and purity, we are slightly taken aback by Scripture's praise of Samson. It is no doubt this reason which has led to his relegation from the pulpit to the Sunday-School room. It's a good story to encourage children about the mighty power of God as long as we keep to his exploits with the lion and temple porches and spare them from details of Samson's three women. Yet, God allows him a place in the catalogue of faithful ambassadors.

When we translate this point into contemporary Christianity, we begin to see that the brash evangelist who is beginning to enjoy the adulation for himself, can still be used by God. Whereas the faith of Gideon and Barak was gently and imperceptibly coaxed by God, Samson seemed to resist any such divine intervention. His belief in his own strength became total and ceased to be grounded in its source. His sensual desires meant that he became too involved with three females to provide an effective spiritual and political lead to his people. Also his desire for vengeance meant that he took matters into his own hands, unlike Gideon and Barak who both allowed God to go before them.

Clearly, although we can be positive about certain aspects of his life, we mustn't become blinkered. Scripture leaves us in no doubt that the Spirit of God eventually forsook him. We are left to praise a 'what might have been' man rather than the real person. If only the enormous power had been channelled in the right direction. If only his great passion had been extended on love for his God-given charges rather than illicit and demanding affairs. If only his thirst for vengeance had been changed into a God-inspired desire for justice.

His life and failure inspire us all to encourage the flashy extrovert to use his gifts for the glory of God. Yet so often we stand on the touchline and wait for the proof of the Spirit of God leaving such a person. Then we say 'I knew that would happen.'

If only we could spot such Christians before they turn in on themselves and carry out a vendetta of vengeance against Christians who have misunderstood them. If only we could encourage such people to exert their power and charisma for God, rather than for themselves. If only we could release them to show affection and love for the whole of God's people instead of having exclusive relationships which ultimately damage their witness. Then they would be people with huge faith and some failure, instead of being like Samson who was a man of minute faith and huge failure. If only . . .

CHAPTER FIVE

JEPHTHAH THE RASH

(JUDGES 11)

On dangerous ground (*Judges 11:1–5*)

Jephthah was annoyed. The elders of his tribe, who years before had done nothing to stop his enforced exile, were now standing in front of him at his hideaway. His annoyance didn't stem from the fact that they had found his base in the hills of Tob. Nor was it that they were offering him the opportunity to lead the Israelites against the hated forces of Ammon. In fact, that rather pleased and flattered him. What annoyed him most was that there seemed to be no remorse. Not one apologized for their failure to help him in the past. They had come with their matter-of-fact attitude expecting him to accept their offer.

He still smarted as he looked at them and remembered the ignominy of being driven out of his home. The callousness of his older brothers who had seen him as a threat to their ageing father's will; the disclosure of his illegitimacy, something he had always feared and now knew to be true; the harsh things said by elders who should have helped the young Jephthah, but instead had fuelled the simmering hatred of the village. All these memories burnt up inside him as he considered his reply.

It was not only *his* emotions which were running high. A different set of emotions were also highly charged in the elders. Despite their calm presentation of the carefully rehearsed offer, they had all felt nervous as they made their way to Tob. They had been conscious with every step towards Jephthah's lair, that they were leaving the security of their own community where they were undisputed leaders. Instead they were going into a domain where a man who had been banished from their jurisdiction now held sway. Over the years he had been joined by a large group of brigands. They had built up a reputation in the region of Tob for their fearless deeds. Jephthah himself was regarded as a mighty man of valour. On the journey to the caves, the elders had tried to smother the rising fears of potential danger. What if Jephthah ordered his warriors to attack them? What if, far from being pleased to accept their placatory offer, he was furious at their intrusion onto his territory?

Jephthah was indeed furious, but expressed his anger through his tongue rather than his sword.

'Didn't you hate me and drive me from my father's house?' he asked. 'Why do you come to me now you are in trouble?'

The spokesman of the elders did not consider it wise to encourage an argument. Jephthah was aroused and it would be far better to remain safe.

'Nevertheless, we are returning to you now,' he said. That was probably the closest he would get to an apology.

Jephthah realized this was his moment. There had been general talk about him leading the Israelites. Now he swooped in for the kill.

72

'Suppose you take me back to fight the Ammonites and the Lord gives them to me – will I really be your head?'

The elders were cornered.

'The Lord is our witness: we will certainly do as you say.'

And so Jephthah the despised became their undisputed leader.

Here we go again (*Judges 11:6–16*)

The elders were pleased with the outcome. As they scrambled back to the security of their homes they were filled with optimism. Jephthah, they were sure, was the man to lead Gilead and possibly the whole of Israel against the Ammonites.

For eighteen years the people had known the constant attacks of Ammon. They had also sensed the displeasure of God. Whereas in the past he had always responded when his people had begged forgiveness, it had been very different this time. The spiritual leaders were convinced that God was withdrawing his presence. They had given this chilling message to the anxious people. God, they believed, was saying to them 'When the Egyptians, the Amorites, the Ammonites, the Philistines, the Sidonians, the Amalekites and Maonites oppressed you and you cried to me for help, did I not save you from their hands? But you have forsaken me and served other gods, so I will no longer save you. Go and cry out to the gods you have chosen. Let them save you when you are in trouble.'

The people responded by ridding their hills of the detested idols. They threw themselves on God's mercy, giving one last-gasp cry that he would rescue them quickly. Whilst God eventually responded to their prayer, it is important to remember the long time gap.

In that period God allowed the people to experience the

result of their sin. For too long they had seen God as a soft touch. If they came running he would relent. A few well-chosen bows, several vows and many tears were the ingredients for their regular act of repentance. God always obliged, often in a spectacular vein. For a while the people would continue their new-found religion. Attendances leapt up at the altars and the future looked rosy. Then as time went on they went back to the hills, erected new idols, organized huge festivals in honour of the fertility gods and forgot all about the God of Israel.

Because of this God withdrew and allowed them to experience the logical conclusion of their own position. 'Go and cry out to the gods you have chosen. Let them save you when you are in trouble.'

Fortunately for Israel, God's displeasure did not last for ever. The writer of Judges informs us that he could bear the indignation no longer. The indignation of seeing men, made in his own image, being slaves to idols of their own making. Eventually he heard their repentant cry and sent a deliverer.

The deliverer God sent was Jephthah. A man who for many years had been discarded by his own people, yet who, in his exile, had thought greatly about his God and his people. God was now ready to reinstate and use him.

God's ordinary man

Jephthah's background was embarrassing to the socially refined of Israel. They would possibly have been warned about asking searching questions about his father and mother. That was best deleted from the curriculum vitae. So, too, was the large section about the years spent in the hills of Tob with his large number of freebooters. Cocktail parties with the new general of Israel's army could in fact be very delicate affairs. It would be far better to take the initiative and concentrate on his military prowess rather then prise the facts from him. In any case, all those years in the backwater of Tob would mean that he was not used to meeting with distinguished people. It may be that he would blurt out all kinds of information and embarrass the entire party if he were allowed to control the conversation.

Such snobbery exists in today's world and God delights in using 'also rans' of society, changing them into people of faith and confounding the snobbery and sensibilities of Christians. How many churches would feel comfortable about Mr Jephthah in a position of leadership? How many Christians with a background similar to that of Jephthah spend years covering up the facts of their history, mortally afraid that some well-meaning Christian may one day discover the truth about them and disown them for ever? Such Christians need to rediscover the fact that God chose to perform his greatest act in the squalor of a cave crammed with animals and filled with their stench. The birth of his one and only begotten Son was shrouded with the paternal fear that he might be illegitimate.

The modern church must rediscover that God's criteria for people of faith are different from society's. He does not ask for well-heeled, well-spoken graduates to lead his church. He is looking for people who have inside them a living and vibrant faith. As the story unfolds, we will discover that Jephthah possessed such a faith. God does not worry about the appearance or the history of the earthen vessel, he is more concerned about the glory inside.

If Jephthah's background shocks our Christian sensibility it is more than likely we will struggle with the nature of his call. He did not have Moses' overpowering experience of God at the burning bush. Nor did he see the temple filled with the glory of God as Isaiah did many years later. Nor was he entertained to the magnificent aerial display of God's glory which was to reduce Ezekiel to prostrate fear. Even Gideon had been shaken to the roots by the appearance of the angel and the commission to go and deliver Israel. Samson's call, mediated through his parents, had been totally spiritual in essence. Jephthah's call appears as human as his birth.

The elders of Gilead were concerned about the movement of Ammonite troops into Israel and asked each other who they could approach to lead the Israelites against Ammon. It was in the course of this conversation that the name of Jephthah appeared. The elders recounted what they had heard about the exile's exploits with his men. In that very human setting they decided to swallow their pride and pluck up the courage to ask Jephthah to become their leader. Indeed the humanity of the story is reinforced by Jephthah's response. It is not many Christian leaders who can claim that their calling to God's ministry was accompanied by a blazing row! Jephthah's certainly was. Yet, there was obviously a conviction that despite the frustration caused by the reappearance of elders who had once despised him, their plans were of God. That conviction was also shared by them, as together they went to Mizpah and repeated all that they had said before the Lord.

It seems God used Jephthah to remind Christians that human origins and experiences should never be despised. Many wait for the blinding light before they go on to their next adventure for God. They forget the number of people who have been called by God through very human agencies. Barak was called through a word from Deborah. Matthias was called to be an apostle through the toss of a dice. Yet his experience, like Jephthah's, stands alongside the spiritual calls of Ezekiel, Moses and Isaiah as equally authentic.

The thinker of Tob *(Judges 11:11–13)*

The exploits of the brigands of Tob could easily have diverted Jephthah's attention from the deep matters of God. He could have become the archetypal bandit, nursing his own hurt, concerned only for his survival. In fact, we find that his Tob experience was a time of stocktaking. So it has been for countless numbers of believers since. After forty years in the bright lights of Egypt, Moses spent a similar period in the wasteland of the desert. Yet that time was used by God to prepare him for the daunting task of uniting and then leading the Israelites to freedom. Similarly, Paul, after his breathtaking conversion, was taken off centre-stage and moved to the obscurity of the desert. His letter to the Galatian Christians is ample proof of the productive nature of his exile thinking. Even Jesus, after the public spectacle of his baptism where God powerfully proved that this is his Son, was removed to the Jordan desert. There he was tempted and his motives relentlessly analysed by Satan for forty days.

Such periods of removal from the public scene are rarely enjoyable. It is only with hindsight that the man of faith begins to see the purpose of God. There must have been long nights of questions in Tob. Jephthah's history up to that point had been fairly nondescript. Yes, he had fought several battles in the district. He had given some purpose to a group of dispirited no-hopers. Yet all his activity had been terribly localized. At such times he felt again the pain of his own personal story. It was difficult to see how he could ever have any part to play in the purpose of God for Israel.

In that lengthy exile it had filtered through to him how the people of Israel were thinking. He knew how for eighteen years they had cowered under the threat of

Ammon. He began to wonder why. When he thought of their history, and of course his (although at times he felt very little part of it), he saw a God who had delivered them. The story of his people was not one of a great super-power brilliantly marshalled by a succession of outstanding generals. It was rather the tale of a small nation led by startled men who relied completely on their God. He had been their judge. So why wouldn't they let him be their judge now? Their whole history was not one of being aggressive fighters but of peaceably desiring access through lands on their way to the promised land. When the kings had refused and waged war God had given those countries into Israelite hands. If only they would have the same attitude now, Ammon could be defeated.

Besides all this, gods of the Ammonites such as Chemosh had a very bad track record in the league table of spectacular national deliverances. And here were the Israelites, with their God and his stunning statistics, fleeing from Chemosh. It was time somebody in charge threw out the challenge. A straight fight: Chemosh versus God.

Such thinking inspired Jephthah to take the initiative in contacting the king of the Ammonites. Now he was in charge he wanted to know how his opposite number felt. So he sent a letter. It was brief and terse. It simply asked 'What do you have against us that you have attacked our country?'

The king's reply was equally conservationist (no doubt in an effort to protect the world's resources of scrolls). He answered 'When Israel came up out of Egypt, they took away my land from the Arnon to the Jabbok, all the way to the Jordan. Now give it back peaceably.'

The lines were drawn, it was time for the battle to commence. But first, Jephthah had one or two misconceptions he wanted to iron out.

The king's chinks *(Judges 11:14–33)*

After his long period of thinking, Jephthah was amazed that two people could look at the same problem and come to such wildly differing conclusions. Conservation or no, this called for a lengthy memo. How could the king say that Israel had taken away his land. They spent years circling it, asking permission from a succession of kings to enter various territories and trying their hardest to keep out of trouble. Eventually they could pussyfoot no longer. Sihon the king of the Amorites rose up against them. In the ensuing battle God gave the whole area from the Arnon to the Jabbok into their hands. So, far from being aggressive, Israel had been given the land by God.

All this talk of 'Give me back my land peaceably' made Jephthah laugh. Israel had been in the land long before this king of Ammon had appeared. So who was being aggressive?

Jephthah felt it was time for his *pièce de la résistance*. Why don't we come to a bargain? We'll keep what our God has given to us and you can have what Chemosh gives to you.

He waited a long time for a reply. The king didn't even send a compliment slip to acknowledge receipt of the scroll and to say he would give the matter some consideration in due time. Nothing.

So it was time for action. Jephthah and his troops went through Mizpah and advanced against the Ammonites. Chemosh gave a particularly bad performance. Jephthah with the help of his living God routed the Ammonites and captured twenty of their towns.

Piety runs amok *(Judges 11:34–40)*

Jephthah was never afraid of speaking his mind. Words

79

often spilt out of his mouth and thoughts followed later. He had responded impetuously to the elders and had straight away challenged the king when he came to power. Of course, there can often be a thin line between strength and weakness, and, in the case of the elders and the king, his impetuosity had also been a sign of great character and faith.

Before he went into battle he uttered words he was to regret for the rest of his life. Tob had taught him the reality of God in the history of his people. The call of his elders had reminded him that God had also been active in his own story. He now wanted to recognize that fact before he went to war. He didn't want to go into battle in his own strength like the brazen brigands of Tob. He wanted to solemnly state his commitment to God.

So he made his vow to God. 'If you give the Ammonites into my hands, whatever comes out of the door of my house to meet me when I return in triumph from the Ammonites will be the Lord's and I will sacrifice it as a burnt offering.'

No doubt in the clash of swords and the rumble of war Jephthah did not think of his vow. Later, as he made his way home in triumph, there were other things on his mind. He was so pleased to be going to his new home in Mizpah. He was looking forward to the adulation of his wife and daughter. It would also be an added bonus to enjoy the congratulations of his once estranged kinsfolk, the Gileadites.

The news reached home before Jephthah. His wife, daughter and the servants were delighted. The scourge of the Ammonites had now been cleansed from Israel once and for all. They were delighted that their very own Jephthah was responsible for the victory.

'Well done, Daddy' would sound so lame after such a momentous victory the daughter decided to mark his homecoming with something grand. She spent several hours rehearsing her dance routine and the servants helped by providing back-up music on the tambourines.

The message was relayed excitedly. Jephthah had been spotted. He was on his way and would be home any minute. Everyone was unanimous his daughter should be the first to greet him. Perhaps because of his own upbringing he loved his only daughter in a way which all the servants admired. Inside the house the lookouts gave the signal. Jephthah walked towards the house. The tambourinists were ready. The daughter was in front and led the troop. Out she came with a superbly choreographed piece. She gave it all she had and the tambourinists joined in heartily.

Jephthah froze. His beautiful daughter, the dance, the jollity and music all added to his misery. His daughter could not understand the grim expression on his face. She continued her dance and the pulsating rhythm became louder. Jephthah tore his clothes and let out a heart-rending cry. The music stopped. The girl broke off her dance.

Slowly the girl was told all about her father's vow. She fully understood the implications. Her father had often told her about his God. She knew how seriously he took his vows and as far as she was concerned there was no way out. She had just one request and it was to spend two months with her friends. The request was granted and when the time expired, Jephthah carried out his terrible deed.

This finale to the victory of Jephthah chills even the writer of Judges. His whole tone is muted as he recalls only the barest details of the vow. He spares us the gory details of the story and nowhere does he applaud what Jephthah did.

To Jephthah a vow was important. He knew the people of Israel had been censured by God throughout history because they had failed to keep their vows. God had been good to him and had not let him down. He was determined to act in a similar way to God. He had promised. God had kept his side of the bargain; Jephthah was determined to keep his. He had learnt from his youth how Moses had told his people 'This is what the Lord commands. When a man makes a vow to the Lord or takes an oath to bind himself by a pledge, he must not break his word but do everything he said.' Besides, Jephthah also knew he had made this vow of his own free will. Again, God's book had something to say about that. 'Whatever your lips offer you must be sure to do, because you made your vow freely to the Lord God with your own mouth.' He was convinced he had inherited the problems of Israel because they had failed to obey God's word. He did not want to go the same way after all God had done for him.

Whilst Jephthah made his vow because of his great zeal for God, we have to conclude it was his sin to vow so rashly. So often people of faith can read God's word, extract certain truths and miss others. He had seen the section about vows but had missed the meaning of the story of Abraham and Isaac. In that story Abraham, surrounded by nations practising child-sacrifice, is ready at God's command to follow suit. But God shows in a dramatic way that this is not what he desires. Instead, he is led to the alternative sacrifice of a ram. If we ask why God didn't intervene in the same way in the story of Jephthah and his daughter, we have to conclude that, unlike Abraham, he had the benefit of God's mind on the matter as we have in the book of Genesis.

Jephthah's vow was also a mistake because he was adding to the revelation of God. Reading his letter to the king, one is amazed at his grasp of God's dealings in history. Yet on to his authentic understanding of God he patched the pagan practice of human sacrifice. Modern people of the faith can fall into the same trap. It can be so easy to incorporate all kinds of modern humanistic thinking into our basic biblical framework. Jephthah did not have the benefit of other godly men trying to question his vow. So often mistakes are made because men of faith are left to get on with their life of faith by themselves. We need other Christians to force us to question our every action in the light of God's truth.

Man of faith, man of failure

Amidst the tragedy of Jephthah's story, we sometimes forget the positive side of his pilgrimage of faith. His commitment to his vow was born out of a high view of God. God must not be let down at any cost. Such a view condemns our Christian scene where vows are made each week and broken soon after the sermon. Many congregations sing weekly vows to God, thinking only of the tunes. 'O Jesus I have promised to serve thee to the end'; 'Take my life and let it be consecrated Lord to thee, take my silver and my gold, not a mite would I withhold.' All these trip off the tongue as easily as the latest prices in the supermarket. Jephthah's consuming faith challenges our flippant attitude.

His vow also challenges us the other way. Just as we see the positive side, we are also alarmed by the way in which he was unable to see that God did not want him to sacrifice his daughter. That rash vow cost him and his daughter greatly. Sadly, Jephthah's rash is contagious in the Christian world. Many Christians can end up with a God who makes demands on their life over and above those found in Scripture. The young girl who decides she must never marry; the young married man who vows to give away too much of his income, thereby putting the rest of his family under financial strain. The story of Christianity is littered with many other examples of people who have followed a god more demanding than the biblical God and have paid dearly for their mistake.

Jephthah's faith, applauded by the writer to the Hebrews, reminds us that the accidents of birth and prejudices of other people can be overcome by a God who is allowed to work. It reminds us that God is not a deity who works only amongst the clean-shaven, clean-spoken masses of suburbia. He is a God who is equally at work in the forgotten backwater of Tob. In that backwater, Jephthah learnt resilience and fighting qualities which God was to use mightily in the future. In the same way Christ's church must wake up to the fact that God may have great plans for the troublesome member of the youth club, with the shocking language and equally vulgar home-life. By the same token he may have great plans for the well-spoken, polite, eight-'O'-levelled, 'never say boo to a goose' teenager who comes from a long-standing evangelical home. God must be allowed to be God and allowed to work where he will. In the same way, faith must be allowed to be faith, flourishing in all its freshness and vitality.

Jephthah's faith also reminds us that the most powerful analysis of the human condition relies on spirituality rather than intellectualism. Jephthah had not been afforded the luxury of further education. Yet in the midst of his unlikely companions he had time to contemplate on the God of his childhood and his relationship to Israel. His analysis for the king of the Ammonites was overwhelming. It also formed the basis for uniting some of the tribes of Israel and leading them into victory. This element of faith, creating a gritty and powerful analysis of society, is sadly missing in our world. The person, uneducated in the world's eyes, yet immersed in Scripture and the knowledge of God is fast disappearing from our Christian culture. In the past it was quite common to meet people who had learnt to read through the Bible and had thus based their whole analysis of life on its teachings.

Scripture reminds us that such people should be more prevalent than they are. Paul reminds the knowledge-conscious Christians of Corinth that people who are the world's fools can be transformed by God's wisdom. Such a caution needs to be heeded by a church which often fails to listen to such people and expects aspiring ministers to be filled with the knowledge of a humanistic society rather than God's wisdom.

In Jephthah, such a faith united men who had been dispirited for eighteen years. It gave a fresh analysis of history and made them unafraid to speak out against influential governments and rulers. Such a faith, shorn of fear, needs to be proclaimed today.

Battle against background

Although Christian theology underlines the fact that we are accepted by God irrespective of our past history, such a fact is often easier to believe intellectually than to express in everyday living. It is easy for the modern Christian to conceal his past like a skeleton in the cupboard. Bible study groups and informal sharing sessions can be sheer torture as he sweats his way through the praise, hoping no-one will ask penetrating questions about his past life.

Jephthah's story encourages us at this point. A history of banditry and illegitimacy is covered by God as he transforms him into a man of faith. Even during his pilgrimage of faith his brash and unstable background seems to lead him into the rash promise which in turn leads to the death of his only daughter.

The apostle Paul's life also furnishes us with an important

lesson. Looking back in later life, his own postscript was that he had been the chief of sinners. The deaths of many Christians on the route between Jerusalem and Damascus could have haunted his missionary-travel dreams. Yet he was able to cling to the fact that Christ's cleansing of our sin is to be a daily reality rather than an abstact thought.

It is important to note that whilst our background is no barrier to God, he rarely obliterates the lessons such a background can offer. As Jephthah's half brothers rejected and taunted him, he must have learnt resilience and independence. These were to stand him in good stead for his long exile in Tob, his solo effort in rallying the troops and his verbal and physical battles against the king of Ammon.

Similarly, while Paul was to become deeply ashamed of his Jewish intolerance of the Christian sect, his academic training which that background had given him was greatly used by God in his missionary escapades. Paul with his keen Jewish mind was able to match the intellectual gymnastics of his Athenian audience. He was also able to set out a cogent apologetic for the gospel in his widely read letter to the Romans.

Such examples remind us that our past is not something of which we should be ashamed. If in the company of well-spoken Christians we clutch our Gorbals accent and wrap it in a smile of silence, we must remember that such niceties do not trouble our divine maker. Rather, he is able to translate the accident of our birth or the ignominy of our background into the nucleus of a powerful story of faith.

The story so far . . .

Already we have learnt there is no such thing as a stereotype person of faith. The four characters who have walked through our pages are all essentially different. Not only are they different but they have also taught us that characteristics which at first seem depressingly negative can be used by God.

Gideon's inferiority has been fashioned into an unbending faith which banished the Midianites. Barak's hesitancy and Jephthah's embarrassing background were both transformed into positive assets to faith. In the same way, God still managed to prove his power through flippant Samson. These four characters remind us that if our lives are dominated by inferiority, hesitancy, flippancy or an embarrassing history these are not reasons for throwing in the spiritual towel. They also remind us that through our earthly walk of faith we can gain vital insights into the heart and mind of God.

Gideon discovered that his timidity could be emboldened by a God who promised to fill him with his Spirit to such an extent that it appeared to onlookers as though God was clothing himself in Gideon. Barak's hesitancy was kept in check by a God who promised to go before. Such a God did not want to be chained by an individual's preoccupation or controlled by his demands. In a negative sense our men of faith have also taught us the dangers of certain attitudes to God. Samson's God chides us for making him a slot-machine deity, ready to meet our every whim, whilst Jephthah's sorry saga underlines the danger of creating a God who is more demanding than Scripture suggests.

We have seen then, four portrayals of the life of faith. In hearing their stories we have recognized our own battles. We have been encouraged, as we watched them fall, to realize that as God remained faithful to them so he will persevere with us. We have also discovered the delicate balance between our humanity and God's power working in close harmony to produce an authentic life of faith. But we have not finished yet. We have still to meet the indecisive Samuel. But first let me introduce you to a man of deep passion. The sensuous king David . . .

CHAPTER SIX

DAVID AND HIS LOVES

(PASSAGES FROM 1 AND 2 SAMUEL)

Love for Jonathan *(1 Samuel 18:1-4)*

Jonathan must often have craved a deep friendship with
someone roughly his own age. Living as the son of the first
king of Israel had its good points but there were also
disadvantages. He had to keep himself fairly distant from
the rest of the people. Michal his sister was alright, but
then she had her own life to lead and her interests and
ambitions were very different from his. Besides all this,
Jonathan's relationship with his father was very
unpredictable. Saul was prone to moods of manic
depression and jealousy and Jonathan was never sure
whether he was in or out of favour.

It was when his father adopted a young shepherd boy
that life started to take an upward turn. Of course, this
was no ordinary shepherd boy. He had just become the
talk of every Israelite household by slaying the feared
Philistine Goliath. All this had been done without the usual

military apparel that was worn for such a historic battle. Showing total disdain for such court etiquette, he had discarded the armour and relied solely on his sling, a handful of stones and his youthful faith in God.

As soon as Jonathan heard David discuss the battle with his father, he knew that here was someone he wanted as a deep friend. David also found Jonathan a person of like spirit and soon a friendship developed which was to sustain and help them through the troublesome years of the future. For Jonathan the friendship offered a release from the strictures and uncertainty of homelife. For David, it became a solace during the awful years of exile and being hunted by Jonathan's father.

Jonathan was anxious that such a friendship should be confirmed by a suitable ceremony. Having seen his father break many promises, he was keen that the love he and David had for each other should have some tangible expression. And so the two of them made a covenant. We do not know what was said, but no doubt it followed the usual eastern pattern. The two of them would have solemnly declared their love for and commitment to each other. They would have done this over a sacrificed animal. Everything promised would have been uttered in the presence of God. The covenant was binding and every Jew believed that to be unfaithful to a covenant made with another person was ultimately being unfaithful to God.

So the friendship got off to the best possible start. It was recognized and cemented in the presence of the God whom David loved. It was further cemented by Jonathan's gifts to David. Taking off his robe, tunic, sword, bow and belt he gave them all to David. This was a remarkable gesture, as they all symbolized Jonathan's future. Jonathan was the son of the king of Israel and although the monarchy was still in its infancy, it must have been expected and assumed that one day he would inherit the crown from Saul. Yet, in the covenant ceremony Jonathan gave to David all the symbols of his future kingship. In their friendship Jonathan never once expressed any envy of this friend who was to oust him from the throne. In fact, Jonathan actively helped him win the throne and informed him that he believed he should be the king.

It was this aspect of Jonathan's friendship with David which angered Saul. Whilst his response to the popular adulation for David was no doubt fired by his own unstable personality, it was also inspired by his own desire that one day Jonathan should be king. Instead of Jonathan siding with him and trying to eradicate the pretender to the throne, he became a friend of David and often passed on vital information enabling him to anticipate Saul's next move. For Saul, his problems were doubled by the fact that his daughter Michal married David and in the early days of the marriage, she too aided David's escapes from her father. This paternal frustration is expressed in Saul's outburst to his son, when Jonathan tried to encourage Saul to stop hunting David. Saul roared his response: 'You son of a perverse and rebellious woman! Don't I know that you have sided with the son of Jesse to your own shame and the shame of the mother who bore you? As long as the son of Jesse lives on this earth, neither you nor your kingdom will be established. Now send and bring him to me, for he must die!' (1 Samuel 20:30–32)

Dangerous friendship *(1 Samuel 20:1–3)*

It was against the backdrop of this death threat that the friendship between Jonathan and David had to develop. This was no coffee-break relationship which talked about the latest archery competition or where they planned to take a vacation. Like so many of David's relationships in the early days of his life, it had to be conducted on the run.

The running started for David when Saul sent some of his men to his house to take and kill him. Michal, by now David's wife, was forewarned and encouraged David to escape by night. He escaped to Ramah to meet and consult with Samuel. Surely the wise old man of Israel could encourage him and tell him his next move. Even this conversation was interrupted by the news that Saul and his men were fast approaching Ramah. So David moved on and went to seek out his friend. He had three questions for Jonathan. 'What have I done? What is my crime? How have I wronged your father, that he is trying to take my life?'

Jonathan's response was fairly encouraging although perhaps not terribly objective. He was convinced that his father would not really harm David. He was also convinced that Saul would attempt nothing without confiding in Jonathan. David was not so certain. Rather, he told Jonathan that Saul would not tell him everything for fear of upsetting him. David, despite the pleasure of seeing his friend, was depressed by the reality of the situation. As far as he was concerned he was only 'one step from death'.

Friendship jitters *(1 Samuel 20:4-23)*

Realizing that the next day was the beginning of the New Moon Festival, when all those connected with the court were expected to attend the meal, David hit upon a plan of action. Was Saul really out to kill him? Or was it as Jonathan suggested, that deep down he had no such intention? Perhaps all this frantic hunting was no more than an expression of Saul's moodiness and instability. Even so, it would have been too risky to turn up for the meal all smiles and innocence, just in case Saul leapt up from the table and commanded his acolytes 'Off with his head.' So David told Jonathan to spin Saul a yarn about his having to go to Bethlehem to take part in an annual family gathering. If the king had no intention of harming him, then he would accept the story. If on the other hand he had looked forward to this feast as the night when David would have to come to court and walk into a death trap, then he would be furious at the missed opportunity.

Jonathan agreed to play along with the plan. But there was still the slight problem of how to convey Saul's reaction to David. It wouldn't do for him to hang around the court waiting for the latest bulletin. Instead, Jonathan suggested that for the next couple of days he hide in the fields near the rock at Ezel. On the morning of the third day Jonathan would come with a boy from the court. He would aim three arrows toward the large stone in the field as if he were shooting at a target. The boy was to stand between Jonathan and the stone. David had to hide behind the rock out of sight. If he heard Jonathan call to the boy that the arrows had landed in front of him, then he was safe. If on the other hand Jonathan said the arrows had landed behind the boy, then Saul was still out to harm David and he must flee.

In the conversation the nerves of both friends were exposed. David, despite the covenant they had made, began to wonder whether Jonathan really would stand by him. After all, he was aiding David in a fight against his father. Therefore, he said to his friend that if he, David, were guilty of anything against Jonathan's father then he would rather Jonathan kill him now rather than hand him over to Saul. Needless to say the young prince was not happy with either option. He swore to David that whatever Saul's intentions, he would tell him.

Later on, it was Jonathan's turn to become uneasy. He was convinced that one day David would be king of Israel. He was not alone in that belief and felt that it was God's plan for the country. He was happy to help David fulfil that plan. At the moment David was vulnerable, fleeing hither and thither, hiding behind rocks and needing the support of anyone who could help. But what about in the future when God's plan came to fruition and David was the undisputed king of all Israel? Saul would probably be dead. What of Jonathan then? Would David still need him or would he see him as a potential threat? In view of this Jonathan pleaded with his friend to calm his nerves. 'Show me unfailing kindness,' he said, 'like that of the Lord as long as I live, so that I may not be killed, and do not ever cut off your kindness from my family – not even when the Lord has cut off every one of David's enemies from the face of the earth' (1 Samuel 20:14–15).

After this frank discussion there was only one thing they could do to mark the reassurance they have given each other. They made another covenant in which they affirmed to each other and to God that they would maintain their friendship whatever happened.

Spiritual friendship

Jonathan's optimism concerning his father did not last long. Saul was furious that his son could be so blinkered as to fail to see that he was actually plotting his own downfall. Saul confirmed his anger by hurtling a javelin at Jonathan, which mercifully missed. Escaping the flying weapon, Jonathan moved into the field at Ezel to fire his three shots over the boy's head.

David heard his friends's commentary on his archery and knew that he was still a fugitive. His days as a fugitive took him to Nob, Gath, Adullum, Mizpah, Keilah. In every place there were plots, counterplots and betrayal. He finally fled to the hill country of Ziph and it was at Horesh that Jonathan caught up with him again (1 Samuel 23:16–18).

The writer of the book of Samuel informs us that Jonathan found David and helped him to find strength in God (1 Samuel 23:16). Their friendship was not merely religious in the formal setting of a convenant. It also had the dynamic dimension of an ongoing spirituality. It was so easy for David to lose sight of the God he loved. In the early days of this faith he was able to face Goliath in the knowledge that the God who had enabled him to kill a lion and a bear whilst tending the sheep, would also help him against the Philistine giant. It would have been very easy for that faith to have been worn down by the constant harassment of an unstable king trying to slay him. Jonathan must have remembered that his friend had told him he felt just one step from death. And so he came to him with the sole intention of bolstering his faith in God. This is no 'stiff upper lip' chit chat or 'chin up' morale-booster. He realized that David would only have abiding stength to face adversity if it were drawn from the living God.

It is also interesting to note that it wasn't a pious monologue. Unlike Job's so called friends who rattled off their moralistic observations in a cold 'take it or leave it' style, Jonathan, rather than making a speech, helped David to find strength in God for himself. We don't know what he did or said, all we know is that he provided David with the stimulus to rediscover his faith and to feel again the reality of a God who had protected him in the past.

Jonathan also pointed out that God was in control. As far as he was concerned, all Israel knew that one day David would be king. Even the troubled Saul knew this. David must simply trust for the future as he had trusted in the past.

A deep friendship *(2 Samuel 1:17–27)*

It is ironic that David, who spent a great percentage of
his early life staring death in the face, came through
unscathed and eventually ruled Israel. On the other hand,
Jonathan, who had enjoyed the protection of court life was
killed in the battle. He, his father and two brothers were
all slain by the Philistines in the battle of Mount Gilboa.

David, so often moved to write joyous hymns in praise
of God, finds himself penning a lament. The doleful refrain
'how the mighty have fallen' begins and ends his poem.
He was devastated that two men who were as swift as eagles
and as strong as lions now lay slain on the heights of Gilboa.
To David it was far more significant than the mere loss
of Saul and Jonathan. It felt as if the glory of God had been
withdrawn from Israel. That was something only Israelites
should think about. He didn't want such talk to be uttered
in the Philistine towns of Gath and Ashkelon 'Lest the
daughters of the Philistines be glad, lest the daughters of
the uncircumcised rejoice.'

David's eulogy is amazing in that he found time to praise
Saul. Although most of his relationship with the king had
been spent fleeing from him, David was still able to say
that in his life he was loved and gracious. His adulation
of Jonathan is understandably much deeper. He writes:

> 'How the mighty have fallen in battle!
> Jonathan lies slain on your heights.
> I grieve for you Jonathan my brother:
> you were very dear to me.
> Your love for me was wonderful,
> more wonderful than that of women.'

Up to the death of Jonathan, David's relationship with

his wife Michal had been far from usual. Much of his married life had been spent away from home, on the run from Saul. In such circumstances it is perhaps understandable that he could cite his friendship with Jonathan as deeper than that of his relationship with Michal. The absence of Michal was not, of course, the only factor that led to this bold statement. Jonathan's love was unique in many ways. Three times he had instituted a solemn covenant to mark its special nature. He had sacrificed the opportunity of becoming king of Israel for the friendship of David. Many times he had risked serious recriminations from his father by passing on vital information to David. On one occasion his short life was nearly ended by the jealous Saul, who was furious at Jonathan's support for David. It is little wonder that, on hearing the news of Jonathan's death, his friend was so devastated. Against such a backcloth, it becomes more understandable why he could describe Jonathan's love as deeper than that of women.

We live in an individualistic and suspicious age. In such a society we find it difficult to contemplate the love of these two men without immediately raising questions about their sexuality. We find it easier to place people in boxes than to objectively consider their love. David and Jonathan were both 'he men'. Jonathan had led many successful military campaigns; David was a warrior whose zest for life was healthy and boisterous. Yet they needed each other and recognized their need before each other and God. The story of their friendship reminds us that people of faith are never intended to live their lives in isolation. Jesus once sent the disciples out in pairs when he commissioned them to evangelize. Barak needed the support of Deborah before he could fight for God. Jesus himself is depicted in the gospels as having special friends. He did not weep when he saw the dead bodies of Jairus' daughter or the son of the widow of Nain. Yet when he was confronted with dead Lazarus he wept in such a way that the sceptical Jews were all impressed by the depth of his love.

Again, the gospel writers tell us that, whilst Jesus went ministering from town to town with his band of disciples, there were occasions when he opted to be in the company of just three of the twelve. It was Peter, James and John who accompanied him into the bedroom of the dead twelve-year-old girl. The same three accompanied him to the mount of transfiguration and John is described by the writer of the fourth gospel as 'the disciple whom Jesus loved' and elsewhere as 'the beloved disciple'. We are also told that at the last supper he reclined on the breast of Jesus.

All this serves to show that it is perfectly acceptable and part of God's plan for Christians to have deep friendships with members of the same sex. In the case of David, his friendship with Jonathan was a special gift from God. The man of faith would have found it difficult to cope with all the pressures of exile without that God given friendship. In modern Christianity we are often satisfied with fleeting and superficial acquaintants. The chorus says 'Let there be love shared among us, let there be love in our eyes . . . give us a fresh understanding of brotherly love that is real.' David and Jonathan had that understanding. Every man or woman who is going to be used by God needs that same understanding and that gift from God of a friend who sticks closer than a brother.

Man of many loves

David's love for Jonathan was strong because it was constantly brought to God for his blessing. In fact, his love for Jonathan was merely a reflection of his love for God. To understand David's character and his life of faith is to understand love in many of its facets. He loved Jonathan as his own brother and Jonathan in return loved him with a love as deep as the love of a woman for a man. David's love for God was vibrant and dynamic. It filled the many psalms he penned and inspired him throughout his chequered career. But that love was again a reflection, in this case, of God's love for him. Because God loved David, he was able to accept himself as someone who was special and important. This love for himself gave him confidence and the ability to accept himself in every difficult situation.

These three loves, of Jonathan, God and himself, fired David and inspired him to live a life of faith which earned God's plaudit that he was a man after his own heart. Yet, as we have already seen in many of our men of faith, a stength can also be a weakness. For David his love of himself, whilst being something which liberated him, also ultimately ensnared him. On many occasions he tried to preserve his life by his own efforts instead of trusting God and this led to deceit and insensitivity to other people.

The most famous example of David's love becoming a weakness and leading to his downfall, is his adultery with Uriah's wife Bathsheba. David was a man with a huge heart and in that huge heart was a lot of love. Sometimes that love was directed to the right channels and other times it was misdirected. It is through this theme of love that we consider David's life of faith. A love for Jonathan, God, self and Bathsheba.

Love for Self
Take me as I am

Unlike Gideon, David was not given to bouts of self-doubt. As a man he was supremely confident. So confident that as a teenager he could take on Goliath. In later life, his confidence enabled him to live as a fugitive and escape from town to town. After that period of exile he was able to unite and lead Israel into a period of great prosperity. Such feats cannot be achieved by a man who is constantly looking in the mirror and lamenting his wretchedness. The Old Testament documents testify to David being confident without being conceited or aloof.

His confidence came primarily from his faith in the God who would deliver him. But that faith also expressed itself in his view of himself. Because God loved him, David considered himself special. His God loved him as a shepherd loves his sheep. As we have already seen, his God delighted in David. These beliefs formed the basis for David's confidence. God loved him so much he must be special. If he were special to God then David should love and accept himself. Ripped out of context such a statement can sound brash and conceited. Yet in the presence of God, self-love and acceptance is vital for any person of faith. Gideon struggled with his faith because he had such a low view of himself. David's faith was strong for the opposite reason; he had a high view of himself and his worth and potential before God.

Many Christians fail to achieve their potential for God because they have such a low view of themselves. Bogged down by their looks which are not as breathtaking as those of others in the youth fellowship or Christian union, young Christians can often lose any vision of what they could achieve for God. Older Christians can suffer in similar ways by failing to offer themselves for Christian service within their church fellowship because they are convinced that Mr X or Mrs Y could do the job better than they. Both groups need to respect their God-given uniqueness and remember that as far as God is concerned they are as precious to him as the apple or pupil of his eye.

Such encouragement is not restricted to the Old Testament. Paul's letters are full of reference to what people who had been aliens to God's promises can now be, through what Jesus has achieved on the cross. He informs the Ephesians that they must lift themselves beyond the clogging confines of life in Ephesus and remind themselves that they are seated with Jesus in heavenly places. This is fighting talk for people who are prone to beat their breasts and call themselves 'worms of the dunghill'. The cross of Jesus assures such that they are important to the extent of his sacrificing his very life. Such giving must release them to accept their own worth before God. Although David lived centuries before Christ's supreme gift, he had enough knowledge of God's goodness to accept his self-worth and importance. It was this which enabled him to be confident in the face of every adversity. Yet, as so often happens, the strength of a man of faith can often become his weakness. So it was for David. His love for himself, instead of being grounded in the character of God, sometimes became purely selfish. At such times he lost sight of God and tried to protect himself with his own ingenuity. This led to deceit and, in one terrible instance, the death of eighty-five innocent priests.

A little lie costs lives *(1 Samuel 21:1–9; 22:6–23)*

Ahimelech the priest shivered with fear. Why had David the mighty warrior come to see him? David's answer frightened him even more. 'The king charged me with a certain matter and said to me "No-one is to know anything about your mission and your instructions." As for my men, I have told them to meet me at a certain place. Now then what have you to hand? Give me five loaves of bread, or whatever you can find.'

David's answer is shot through with lies. It is the top of a slippery slide down which he rode time and again. Hungry from his days of trying to give Saul the slip, he worked on the assumption that Ahimelech the ageing priest would not realize that he was out of favour with King Saul. To tell him that he was running from the king might mean that the priest would not give him any food. So he spun a yarn about being on a secret royal enterprise.

David no doubt thought about his strategy as he approached the priest's dwelling. A little lie would probably provide the five loaves he needed to get through the rest of the day. Surely God would wink at this little indiscretion. Yet as events turned out, this 'little lie' was to cost the lives of Ahimelech, eighty-five other priests and the destruction of the priestly town of Nob.

In the priest's house that day was Doeg the Edonite. Doeg was a slipery character in charge of all Saul's shepherds. Anxious to keep in with Saul, he quickly realized that David was on the run from the king. As far as he was concerned, what the priest was doing in harbouring and helping David was little short of treason. He missed no opportunity in relaying the message back to headquarters. It resulted in Ahimelech and the rest of the priests appearing before Saul. The incensed king ordered his guards to kill them. Feeling distinctly sorry for the godly men, they refused to carry out his orders. It was the ruthless Doeg who ultimately carried out his wishes and slew all the priests.

It is apparent from later events that David seeing Doeg, guessed that he would inform Saul. In spite of this, he continued to trick the priest knowing full well that he may be punished by the king. At no time did he give Ahimelech the opportunity to choose his own course of action. The lie kept growing until it destroyed many lives.

The jester who wasn't funny *(1 Samuel 21:10–15)*

Just as in the early days faith in God had come easily to David, as he left Ahimelech's house in Nob, he found that something else came easily. Lying became his trademark. David's love for himself ceased to be grounded in God. It became crass self-preservation at all costs. Having resulted in the death of the priests it now led him to deceive Achish the king of Gath.

Moving from Nob, thinking of the implications of Doeg's presence at the priest's house and the inevitability of Saul renewing his hunt for him, David decided the only course of action open to him was to try and attach himself to a powerful ruler. He found his way to the Philistine ruler at Gath and enroled as a mercenary fighter. It was not very long before the court servants became uneasy. Chatting in the domestic quarters they sized up the new member of staff. One of them recognized him as David of Israel. The recognition put the entire staff off their food. What on earth was Achish thinking about in employing a man such as David? The Philistines were constantly at war with Israel, yet here was their Philistine king allowing one of the Jewish military folk heroes free access to his court. One of the servants even remembered the song some of the Israelites sang at their celebration dances. He couldn't recall all the words, but remembered that the chorus praised David:

'Saul has slain his thousands,
and David his tens of thousands.'

The unease gradually percolated through to David. He

103

decided his only hope was to feign madness. And so as the rumours flew around the court, they were about a man who stood gibbering at the door post, sinking his teeth into the woodwork and allowing his spittle to run down his beard whenever he attemped to eat his food. Achish was incredulous when the servants told him who his new fighter really was. Instead of a young man with a great physique and military bearing he found himself talking to a babbling fool whose eyes rolled around in his head whenever the king tried to hold his attention. The king had had enough and called his servants. 'Look at the man! He is insane! Why bring him to me?' he said. 'Am I so short of madmen that you have to bring this in front of me? Must this man come into my house?'

David's desire to save his own skin had consumed him to such an extent that he had lost his relationship with God. Confronted with the problems at Nob and Gath he took the matter into his own hands. This is in marked contrast to the man who spent time in prayer asking God whether he should attach Keilah. It is also in marked contrast to the young David who, in facing Goliath, could say 'The Lord who delivered me from the paw of the lion and the paw of the bear will deliver me from the hand of this Philistine.' David forgot that yesterday's faith would not suffice for today. In its place he found selfishness and deceit; a deceit which was to lead him in to even deeper water with the same king of Gath.

Whose side am I on? *(1 Samuel 27 & 29)*

After a lengthy period being hunted, David decided to return to Achish. This time he went with his six hundred Adullumites. We are not told the details but clearly he and his men entered into some kind of pact with the Philistine ruler. The pact allowed David and all the warriors and their families to settle in Gath. It was a dangerous policy indeed and is another example of David preserving his own life in his own way, instead of seeking God's will.

David and his men were sent on various military sorties against the Geshurites, Girzites and Amalekites. Trying to curry favour with Achish and also attempting to reassure him that he was now truly on his and the Philistine's side, David slipped again and lied to the king. He and his men would completely destroy the Amalekite townships and David would return to Gath. On being questioned about his day's work, David, knowing that he had left no survivors who could blow his cover, would tell the king that he had spent the day attacking and destroying townships belonging to the people of Israel. Again it seemed a harmless little lie and was heavily laden with irony. David was surely not harming anyone, but instead was securing the future for himself and his family with the Philistine ruler.

Naturally, Achish was delighted that David who had once thrilled Jewish hearts was now becoming odious to his people. He believed David's word and trusted him implicitly. For a whole year David kept up the deception and enjoyed the adulation that greeted each fresh lie. Then the whole enterprise backfired badly.

Achish decided it was time to rally all the kings of Philistia and with the amassed troops, march against Israel. He assumed that such an enterprise would cause no problems for his new ally, as David had already spent much of his last year destroying Jewish settlements. David was now well and truly trapped. The man who had been told many times by the people and by Jonathan that he would one day rule Israel as God's anointed ruler, was now preparing to wipe them off the face of the earth. David had no alternative, so he and his men marched in the rear of the Philistine advance against the Jews.

Fortunately for David, God intervened through circumstances. The commander of the Philistine army had spent most of the morning hearing complaints from his officers. They couldn't believe Achish could be so gullible. In the end, he had no alternative but to confront the king with the situation. Achish's response was fairly naive. As far as he was concerned, David had been a faithful servant for the past year and he was convinced would continue to serve them in the ensuing battle. The commander would not be placated and said 'Send the man back, that he may return to the place you assigned him. He must not go with us into battle, or he will turn against us during the fighting. How better could he regain his master's favour than by taking the heads of our own men?' Mercifully for David, the king was finally convinced and sent all the Hebrews back to their camp at Ziklag. He was thus spared the indignity of slaying his own people. It was no doubt God's providential intervention prompting the Philistine commanders to complain in the way they did. Otherwise David's unhealthy love for himself could have destroyed all the future plans for him to consolidate and lead the people of Israel. David's penchant for telling little lies had a habit of producing huge problems as the incidents with Ahimelech and Achish testify. Yet even those seem miniscule compared to the problems created by his illicit love affair with Bathsheba.

Love for Bathsheba
Time on his hands *(2 Samuel 11:1-5)*

Saul and Jonathan were dead and David was on the throne.

Days of furtive exile seemed almost to belong to another person. He was now in the strange position of being able to send his armies to do battle for him. He had proved himself as a warrior, now he was going to enjoy himself as a king. Of course he kept in touch with his men at the front through the odd dispatch, but on the whole he rather enjoyed the luxury of the palace and the knowledge that the battle against the Ammonites was going well and was being masterminded by the competent Joab.

Of course, for a man who's been used to a nomadic 'on the run' existence, even a life of luxury can have its drawbacks. One evening David was bored. Strolling on his flat roof he must have allowed himself a wry smile as he contrasted what he now had, with his years as a penniless fugitive from King Saul.

Looking down on the houses of his subjects, his attention was caught by a beautiful lady taking a bath. The servant who was summoned must have found it a strange request, but he didn't bat an eyelid as he went to discover the name of the lady David was watching. It was Bathsheba, wife of Uriah, a man congratulated by the biblical chronicler as a fighter of mighty valour. Indirectly she had strong military connections. Her father Eliam is also mentioned in the list of important military figures in Israel and he and Uriah were both fighting the Ammonites at Rabbah.

It was still not too late for David to get off a slide which was going to be even slipperier than the one he tumbled down with Ahimelech and Achish. He could simply thank God for the gift of beautiful bodies and return to his wife Abigail. Unfortunately, David began to think that as the monarch of Israel what he commanded would be granted. So he sent servants from the palace to convey Bathsheba from her house to the king. That night they slept together and later the news was conveyed to David that the one night stand had resulted in a pregnancy.

The people of Israel were strongly opposed to adultery. Basing their response on the Levitical law, they believed that such an act was worthy of the death penalty. Whilst it is unlikely that anyone would have been able to impose such a sentence on David, it seems that he was aware of the seriousness of what he had done and so he tried desperately to cover his tracks.

Cover up *(2 Samuel 11:6–27)*

It was quite clear that David was the father of the child. Bathsheba had just finished being ceremonially unclean due to menstruation and therefore there was no way in which her husband could be responsible for the pregnancy. Besides, he was away at Rabbah fighting for his king and country. David acted quickly. If only Uriah were around, that would at least help people to assume the child was his.

When Uriah arrived from the battlefield, David pampered him with questions, good wishes and gifts. He still had one slight problem. No self-respecting Jew would lie with his wife whilst he was actively involved in military service. Washing the feet was a symbolic gesture that they were absolved from abstinence and could enjoy their conjugal rights. So David told Uriah 'Go down to you house and wash your feet.'

Early the next morning David, orchestrating events from his palace, was informed by one of his servants that Uriah did not go home to Bathsheba. Furious, he sent for the soldier and asked him to explain himself. Uriah replied 'The ark and Israel and Judah are staying in tents, and my master Joab and my Lord's men are camped in the open fields. How could I go to my house and eat and drink and lie with my wife? As surely as you live I will not do such a thing.'

Uriah was anxious to get back to the battle. David had other ideas. By now, the invitations were wearing thin and there was more of a veiled command in his statement that he would like Uriah to stay another night and return to Rabbah the next morning. That evening he was wined and dined by the king and when David was convinced that Uriah was in no fit state to drive his chariot, he sent him home.

The servant's bulletin in the morning was as depressing as on the previous day. Once again Uriah did not go home, but chose instead to sleep with his servants at the gate.

David by this time had got everything out of perspective. The villain of the piece was not himself, as he should be, but innocent Uriah. He must be killed at all costs. To put this into effect he sent a note to Joab. Simple and stark, it stated, 'Put Uriah in the front line where the fighting is fiercest. Then withdraw from him so that he will be struck down and die.'

Joab's next dispatch to the king contained news of the battle, yet David was interested only in one line. It read 'Also, your servant Uriah the Hittite is dead.'

Exposure

David had controlled and taken over many people in his quest to satisfy his desire for Bathsheba. First he had taken her over. She had been dragged along in a sordid story of plot and counter plot. She had become involved in a story which resulted in the death of her husband. His death, in turn, had resulted in the death of many other innocent soldiers. In order to stage-manage his murder, Joab had sent many soldiers to storm the walls of Rabbah. The experienced commander had known all along that they would all perish.

Joab himself had been controlled by David and must have wondered why he had to take this drastic action against Uriah. The king was contented that he had covered himself. The servants would have put two and two together and guessed what was happening but then they were unimportant. They would only gossip amongst themselves. The truth would be submerged and now David could enjoy his latest acquisition. After she had wailed and worn her widow's weeds for a while she made her way to the palace and Bathsheba became the king's new wife.

Sadly for David, the matter did not rest there. Whilst everyone else continued about their business and commented on how pleasing it was that the sad story of Bathsheba had such a happy ending, one man was battling with his conscience. Nathan the prophet discovered what had happened, not from indiscreet mutterings of others but through a direct message from his God. He knew what he had to do.

Story with a twist *(2 Samuel 12:1–14)*

Nathan had a gift for telling stories. David listened attentively. A rich farmer lived near a poor farmer. The poor man had no assets except one ewe lamb. One day the rich man had a surprise visitor. Planning a huge feast for the evening, he decided his servants could do that new lamb recipe they'd found. Looking around his livestock he had a brilliant idea. Why run down his stocks? Why not seize the ewe lamb from the old man next door? That's precisely what he did.

David was outraged. 'The man ought to die,' he thundered. Nathan stage-managed the dramatic pause brilliantly. Looking into the king's face he said, 'You are that man.'

Repentance *(Psalms 32 and 51)*

For days David refused food. It felt as if his body were wasting away. As he lay on his bed he often wept for long periods. Suddenly he saw the whole story in a new light. He had destroyed the marriage of Bathsheba and Uriah and in his sensuous desire for her had actually killed her husband.

There was a need to take stock. The God who had inspired him in his early days seemed a million light years away. David knew who had moved. It wasn't God. He was still there trying to communicate with his errant child.

David wrote two psalms which capture his anguish over the Bathsheba affair. In one of them (Psalm 51) he asks God to create in him a pure heart. He knew that he had sinned primarily against God. He was confident that he had silenced all other characters in the plot but he had not bargained on the anger of God. What David had done had displeased him greatly. The nights of weeping and days of being off his food were merely symptoms of the fact that his realtionship with God was not right. It was that relationship which had formed the foundation for the great exploits of his youth. If he were to know God's blessings again, that relationship must be re-established. And so he pleaded with God:

> 'Cleanse me . . .and I shall be clean;
> wash me and I shall be whiter than snow.
> Let me hear joy and gladness;
> Let the bones you have crushed rejoice.
> Hide your face from my sins

111

and blot out my iniquity.
Do not cast me from your presence
or take your Holy Spirit from me.
Restore to me the joy of your salvation.'

In the other psalm (32) he celebrates the forgiveness God gave him after his repentance. He was able to sing that the man whose sins are covered is happy. Before they could be covered they needed exposing by Nathan, but now they had been confessed in the presence of God he could hold his head up high. David had got things mixed up. He thought that as long as no-one knew what he had done he would be happy. He revealed in his psalms of repentance that the opposite is true. It actually doesn't matter if the whole world knows and for ever exposes his sin, so long as God covers his sin and forgives his transgression. Ultimately, that is all that matters.

Passion and faith

So far most of our men of faith have been a mixture of mild panic and hesitancy – with the one notable exception of Samson whose flamboyancy destroyed many people and almost as many religious principles. It has been a welcome change to meet King David whose passion for life is tempered by deep sensitivity.

Society often distinguishes between acceptable and unacceptable sources of passionate commitment. It is totally acceptable to whoop with delight when Ian Rush scores a hat trick, or Wimbledon lift the trophy at Wembley. It is equally acceptable for very ordinary men and women to chant for an entire ninety minutes the names of their local heroes. Somehow, passion in Christian circles is somewhat frowned upon. It is alright to be head-over-heels about our exam results or passing or diving test at the first attempt, but to be adulatory at the communion table is somehow deeply embarrassing.

David reminds us that such joy is possible as an expression of our faith. He scales a wall in the middle of a battle and sees that act as a celebration of the life and faculties God has given him. His whole life is enveloped in a circle. God loves him and he loves God. As he thinks of his life, he begins to think of God's love for him. And so he pulls the circle further around himself and shouts unashamedly 'I love you Lord.'

Such feelings are uttered by a 'macho man'. Often, outsiders' opinions of Christians are rather unflattering. A class of fourth formers were asked to create a photofit picture of a typical Christian. The pupil who put up his hand first, spoke for the entire class. As far as he was concerned, Christians were wimpish looking people, normally thin, pasty faced with thick national-health glasses. Nine times out of ten, they would suffer from acne and be hugely apologetic about everything they did.

The class was amazed to hear the story of David, a man who expressed his humanity fully, yet was deeply spiritual. In the same way, Jesus himself was not afraid of tackling society. He was constantly battling against the Pharisees and showed his intense anger with the authorities when he overturned the merchants' tables in the temple. Two of Jesus' followers were also men who expressed their humanity in striking ways. Simon, before he met Jesus, had been a member of the Jewish terrorist movement known as Zealots. We do not know any specific details of his political career, but we can imagine that to be a member of such a fervent group, he must have been a fairly fearless individual. Simon Peter was also a physical man. Confronted by the temple police in the garden of

Gethsemane, he leapt to the defence of Jesus, brandished a sword and chopped off Malchus' ear.

We are not calling for Christians to join outlawed terrorist groups or carry weapons into praise and fellowship meetings. But such stories remind us that many of the earliest followers of God were real men and women. Christian faith does not demand we rip out any vestiges of human passion. Simon Peter's passion was refined by Christ so that he could later celebrate a living and lively hope in his first letter to the persecuted church. David's passion was also constantly kept in check by his awareness of God's presence and love. It is indeed exciting to imagine David's barrack room full of passionate tales of what God was doing in the world rather than lewd stories and bawdy songs. Just as God could use the hesitancy of Barak and the inferiority of Gideon, he can also use the passionate humanity of people like David. We must nurture not smother such passion in Christians so that their humanity becomes an authentic demonstration of their passion for life and God. Such was David's humanity.

Coping with failure

It is always a temptation for a man or woman of faith to feel that once they commit sin, it is impossible for them to continue in the Christian life. The histories of individual churches are full of stories of young Christians who have slipped from a position of leadership to one of obscurity because of a particular sin they have committed.

David's story reminds us that the individual Christian can be restored into a right relationship with God. The cross, with its promise of instant forgiveness and salvation, must be as significant a symbol throughout our Christian life as it was in the beginning. The blood of Jesus Christ which cleansed us from all our sin and enabled us to enter the family of God on the day of our conversion, still has the power to cleanse and forgive daily. Just as inferiority and hesitancy can be great obstacles in the life of faith, so can previous sin.

The man who appeared on British television informing the audience that although he was a convicted murderer, he was now converted and contemplating entering the Christian ministry, captured more of the heart of the Christian gospel than all those who posted their outraged feeling to the BBC and magazines. Like David, once forgiveness had been sought and granted, such a man is allowed to take his place again in the Christian community.

It is a great temptation to think that such rehabilitation is instant and magical, as if somehow God could bring back Uriah from the dead and banish the baby from Bathsheba's womb. Of course, David was totally forgiven, so much so that God was prepared to call him a man after his own heart. Yet the reality of his sin and the repercussions of his actions were with him for the rest of his life. The child born to Bathsheba died as a seven-day-old baby. David's experience became one long story of suffering: Absalom his son rebelled against him; Ammon, another son, raped Tamar, David's daughter by another wife. And so the story stutters from one tragic incident to another. Yet David is rehabilitated in his relationship with God and knows for the rest of his life the reality of a clean spirit within him. In the final analysis that is surely the most important factor in his life. It releases him to change from a man of failure to one of faith.

Coping with self

We have already tackled issues such as inferiority and

hesitancy through two of our characters. David is totally different in that he appears to have a very balanced view of himself. His love for himself never verges on vengeance and brutality as it does in the story of Samson. His whole demeanour is held together by the interrelationship of love for God, self and others. Samson did not seem to possess such a unity.

Clearly, David's self-love begs the question: In the Christian community where we are called to consider others better than ourselves, how can we contemplate applauding someone who loves himself? If such love predominates then clearly it is wrong. It becomes brash, boastful and unbearable. For David, it was clearly the basis on which the rest of his personality was built, rather than its sum. As we have already seen, that very base was only possible because he realized God loved him so much.

Many Christians fail to love others or to carry out tasks of faith for God, because they cannot accept their own loveliness before God. The fact that God delights in me, hovers around me like an eagle hovering under and above its young, leads me like a shepherd leading his sheep and watches my going out and my coming in, should liberate me to a fresh understanding of my worth before God. The cross with all its horror and shame becomes a symbol of my own self-worth.

God loved me so much he died for me. When I accept such love and translate it into self-love, I cease to be concerned about the way other people respond or relate to me. If they reject me it doesn't matter because, as far as God is concerned, I am the apple of his eye. Such confidence will equip me for any task of God and any expression of faith. As I go into the unknown I will be confident in my own value as a person and God's love for me. It will inevitably affect the way I treat others, as they too are special to God.

Such faith in self is very different from the one which is celebrated by the media and advertising chiefs. According to that view, my confidence is in my body. I must jog to feel good and use certain deodorants to have a good conversation with a stranger. I must feel slim, think slim, eat slim and stay slim. I must buy 'colour me beautful' manuals so that I wear the right clothes, I must go on to a high-fibre diet so that my skin shines and my teeth glisten.

For David, faith in himself emanated from the inside. When his heart was clean, he could hold his head up high. The body which will eventually decompose can never be the source of such faith, but if the heart is right then it will affect our bodies as the inner-person causes the outer-person to skip and shout 'I love you Lord.'

Bring on the child

All our heroes of faith have been fairly unlikely people. They have either been too hesitant, too brash, too rash or too sinful by human standards. Our next character appears as a child who knows little about God. Although he grows into a man who is greatly respected by his contemporaries and later generations, he still often fails because of his hesitancy and caution. So, let's meet Mr Samuel.

CHAPTER SEVEN

SAMUEL: THE FAITHFUL CHILD AND HESITANT MAN

(1 SAMUEL 3, 7, 16)

The boy had tossed and turned all night. The half light, which was neither night nor morning, danced menacingly on the walls. All night he had been aware of those eerie nocturnal shapes. They added to the tension of the past few hours. He had disturbed the old man twice. Both times he had denied calling. Yet Samuel was convinced he heard someone shouting. The drama of the evening was getting to him. Had he heard a voice? Or was he so frightened, he was hearing voices in his mind?

It would be better to get up and light all the lamps. At the moment it was quiet. Fear fastened him to the mattress. He was afraid that movement of any sort would somehow disturb the peace of the past few moments. He lay motionless, willing the dawn to come.

In this state, he began to think of his mother and father. His memories of them were patchy, yet happy. He could just remember those first four years at home. With titbits of conversation gleaned from his mother's visits, he could construct a happy childhood. He knew his father loved him and every time his mother visited, it was clear she doted on him. Many times she had retold the story of the way she had promised him to God and fulfilled that promise when Samuel was born. He knew he was special. He knew, too, that these were troubled times for Israel. He also knew how his father hoped that one day he would replace Eli and become God's spokesman for Israel. That thought pleased and frightened him. Right now the last thing he thought about was leading Israel. He wanted to go home. In the dim light of the flickering lamp he could just make out the sleeping frame of the old man. Samuel had watched him slow down over the past year. He had heard many snippets from disgruntled pilgrims. They were obviously dissatisfied with his leadership, horrified at the immoral behaviour of Hophni and Phinehas his two sons, and even more disgusted that Eli had failed to take any action.

Yet Samuel had happy memories of the old man. He had been kind to him, almost like a father. He had taught him all the ritual of the tabernacle and instructed him in God's word. Eli had always been impressed by the faith of Samuel's parents and this made him kindly disposed towards the boy. Perhaps, life was not so bad after all in Shiloh. Yes, he was happy here and looked forward to serving God in the future. He was obviously over tired, hence the voices. If only he could get some more sleep he would be fine in the morning. He turned over and closed his eyes tight. He saw his mother busy about the house. The thought of her brought a smile to his face. Slowly but surely he was drifting into sleep. Then it happened. There was no mistaking it. 'Samuel,' the voice said. He sat up. Pinched himself. No, he hadn't been dreaming. What could he do? Who else could be calling him? Eli had denied it and there was no-one else in the tabernacle.

The boy thought for some time. There was nothing else for it. By now he was too frightened to sleep. He would wake Eli and explain he kept hearing voices. Surely the wise old man would have some solution.

His reaction surprised the boy. Samuel had been taught the stories of Israel. He loved Eli telling him about Abraham, Joseph and Moses. So dynamic had been their knowledge of God that he appeared to them and spoke in an audible voice. This had puzzled the boy and as he made his way back to bed, he recalled how one day he asked Eli why God had spoken so often in history but no longer spoke today. The priest had explained that, because there was so much sin in Israel, God refused to speak regularly to his people. The people were so disobedient they only rarely heard God's voice. The answer had made sense, but now it made less sense as Samuel pondered Eli's response. Eli had assured him that he did not call. The voice he had heard three times was none other than the voice of God.

Samuel was overwhelmed by such a thought. Surely Eli must be mistaken. If God had decided to break into society with a message, then he would choose someone else. Why didn't he give it to Eli? Samuel was just a boy. He knew the facts about God and his law, but hearing his voice and understanding his message – that was totally different. He wasn't sure if he would be able to handle such an assignment.

Once returned to his bed, he lay watching the light throw its frantic patterns on to the wall. Suppose Eli was wrong. Perhaps he had spoken more out of hope than knowledge. Maybe the three voices had been in Samuel's head after all.

It wasn't long before all his questions were answered. This time the voice was accompanied by a body. In a vision, Samuel saw the Lord standing before him. He followed the old man's formula and stammered out 'Speak, for your servant is listening.' In the excitement he forgot that Eli had told him to make sure he said, 'Speak, Lord, for your servant is listening.'

If Samuel had been frightened during the uncertainty of the three voices, he was even more alarmed at the end of God's speech. He was left in no doubt that the divine visitation was to predict judgment rather than hope. God was going to destroy the family of Eli so utterly that the ears of those who heard about it would tingle. No large-scale sacrifice by Eli would ever atone for the magnitude of his family's sin. God was going to judge and there was no escape.

Morning now seemed further away than when he was disturbing Eli with talk about voices. The old man was still asleep and Samuel knew he would have to wait until daybreak to share the awful news.

When sunlight finally edged away the dark smudges on the wall, Samuel realized he must get up. He tried to busy himself with the daily routine of the tabernacle. There were lamps to see to and doors to open. It was the doors which disturbed Eli. The pleasantries about the sunrise and the new day couldn't last for ever. Eli soon recalled the events of the troubled night. He wanted to know what God had told Samuel. Fearing the worst he commanded the boy to spare none of the details, lest God should judge Samuel. So the lad told him everything and Eli, almost dispassionately yet with a hint of alarm, said 'He is the Lord; let him do what is good in his eyes.'

Child's faith

Samuel's story is a testimony to God's freedom in choosing his ambassador. At a time when Israel desperately needed a deliverer and a divine message, God did not communicate through a mighty warrior or eloquent speaker but through a child. Moreover the child, writing his own account many years later, confessed that at the time of the divine visitation, he did not know God. He knew the ritual of the tabernacle but did not know the living God. After his obedience in telling Eli everything God had told him, Samuel developed into a young man who was blessed by God. Every word of the young prophet had a power which affected the people of Israel. He was renowned as a man whose words of prediction were fulfilled.

The selection of Samuel reminds us that God's attitude to children is different from those of modern Christians. In many churches children are to be seen and not heard. They are banished from the service when the serious business of the sermon begins. Child commitments to Christ are often treated with severe cynicism by older Christians. Yet God chose to send his message of judgment on Israel and the house of Eli via a young boy. Not just a young boy, but one who had not shown the signs of spiritual understanding, merely a loyalty in carrying out ministerial duties in the tabernacle. This willingness to use such unpromising material is matched in the New Testament by the attitude of Jesus. Surrounded by Jews, who believed that children were beyond the pale as far as spirituality was concerned, he made one stand in front of them and proclaimed that unless everyone expressed the same faith as the child, they would never see the kingdom of heaven.

If we were to take the import of this fact seriously, it would have far reaching effects on our attitude to children, young people and faith. We could begin to see that God does sometimes communicate through the mouths of babes and sucklings. The deep spiritual openness of some youngsters in our churches needs to be nurtured rather than crushed. We would then discover that Christian people of faith do not have to be over forty years of age; they might be under twenty or even ten.

Hannah clearly had such a conviction for her son. For many years she had endured the taunts of the women in her village. She could just about cope with their comments. It was the jibes which came from Peninnah she found hardest. She was the other wife of Elkanah (Hannah's husband) and had been blessed with children. Totally insensitive to Hannah's feelings, she often ridiculed her for her barrenness.

On one occasion at the tabernacle in Shiloh, Hannah prayed earnestly to God. She promised that if she conceived a son she would offer the boy to God for the rest of his life. He would also take the Nazirite vow so that no razor would touch his hair, no strong drink pass his lips and he would never contaminate himself by touching a dead body. Perhaps it was easy to make such a vow when it seemed likely that she would remain barren for life, like a person who promises to give away all his money to charity if he becomes rich, yet knows all along that such a possibility is unlikely. Yet for Hannah the unexpected happened. She conceived and bore a son. His very name represents the depth of her feeling. In naming him 'Samuel' she was affirming that the 'Lord had been exalted'. As far as she was concerned he heard her cry and rewarded her diligence.

When the boy was four years old, that was the time to fulfil her promise to God and Eli. It would have been so easy to change her mind. She could have wrapped up her deep attachment to the boy in high-sounding spiritual language. She could have claimed that God had shown her that Samuel's ministry was to be in his home town amongst his own people, not in distant Shiloh. Or she could have dragged Elkanah into the proceedings and claimed it would be more of a witness and blessing to him if the boy stayed at home and kept the family unit intact. In fact, according to Mosaic law, Elkanah had every right to revoke the vow his wife had made. Yet he stood by her in her promise, and encouraged her to hand over the boy to the ageing priest. Mother and father were both convinced that their son was an unexpected gift from God. To mark their deep gratitude they were determined to consecrate him to the service of God.

Just as Samuel's loyalty to God is a testimony to the fact that God uses very ordinary men of faith, it is also a testimony to the fact that the faith of the parents was rewarded. They kept their promise and dedicated a boy to the service of God. That boy was to grow into an outstanding man of God who united Israel and could later stand with confidence in front of the people and ask them to judge him on every aspect of his life.

Parents need to be reminded that Christian promises made in services of dedication or infant baptism should not be forgotten with the first bite of christening cake. They should also be encouraged that their squawking baby or cantankerous toddler could become a great man or woman of faith. How we need to pray for such transformations.

The man challenges the nation

As Hannah looked back on her life she would have been pleased about her pact with God. She would have seen her promise rewarded greatly in the way her son matured into a great leader. After his early discovery of God and subsequent youthful pronouncements, he became the undisputed judge and spiritual leader of his people. As such he was often approached and encouraged to plead with God on the people's behalf. The first important example of this was when the Israelites were told by Samuel to gather at Mizpah and seek the Lord's help and forgiveness.

Where's God gone? *(1 Samuel 7)*

For some time the Israelites had been aware of the threat from the Philistine army. They were equally aware that as a nation they were dispirited and disunited. There was no great warrior like Gideon or Samson to rally the troops and rid them of their foe. Perhaps worst of all, they no longer felt comfortable when they talked about God. Yes he had acted in the past. But where had he got to? The ark had been abandoned in Kiriath Jearim for twenty years and that fact seemed to symbolize their spiritual plight.

The ark was a box made of acacia wood, overlaid with gold. It housed the tablets of Moses on which the law had been written and Aaron's rod, which had been a spectacular symbol of God's power when Aaron and his brother had visited Pharaoh and the Egyptians.

The ark also had a prominent place in the worship of Israel. It had enjoyed central position in the tabernacle and it was over the ark that God appeared when he talked to Moses and the people.

More recently in their history, Joshua had instructed the people to carry the ark when they crossed the Jordan into the promised land. The crossing had been made when the river was particularly swollen and dangerous. Hoisting the ark above them, the priests had led the way. Amazingly, as soon as they entered the river, the water from upstream stopped flowing. It piled up in a great heap at a point on the river called Adam in the vicinity of Zarethan. Joshua and the people were convinced that the miraculous events in the river were a proof of the presence and power of God. There was nothing magical about the box, but it was a testimony to the fact that God was with them. It is little wonder that when the Jews marched around the walls of Jericho seven times, the procession was again headed by the priests, carrying the ark of the covenant.

The ark represented different aspects of God's dealings. The tablets of Moses reminded them of God's precepts. The fact that he had regularly appeared in the tabernacle over the ark reflected the presence of God with his people. For Joshua and the priests it had been a token of God's power. Precepts, presence and power were all living proof that Israel were God's people and he was their God. The ark was a visual object which underlined that fact.

It is little wonder, then, that the people were distressed by the fact that the ark was housed so far away from the centre of Israel's spiritual life. It had ceased to be a dynamic testimony to God's love for his people. That the ark was not with them, was almost the same as saying that God was no longer with them. Historically the blessings of the ark were hidden far away in the memory and geographically they felt cut off from it. It was not visible in the tabernacle at Shiloh. Services of worship had trundled on without that daily reminder of the nature of God.

In the West, the church of Christ faces a similar crisis. Although Christians oil the machinery of daily and weekly acts of worship, it has to be admitted that there is a deep sense that the dynamic reality of God's presence is locked away in the mists of history. Wesley, Whitfield and the preachers of the Welsh revivals are names from periods which are remembered rather than experienced now.

Similarly, there is a growing sense that just as the dynamic God is locked away in Western history, he seems to be alive and well elsewhere. Culturally, Kiriath Jearim was a long way from Shiloh. Similarly we hear exciting reports of what God is doing in Korea and Brazil, but battle on in our 'corner of the vineyard' with our handful of faithful worshippers expecting little of God and experiencing little from him.

Aware of the terrible situation, the people cried to the Lord. Though his prophet Samuel, he responded to their requests and told them to gather in Mizpah to hear his word.

If . . . then *(1 Samuel 7:1–13)*

Samuel was not given to sweet, soothing sermons. As a child he had to deliver a stinging attack on God's priesthood. Now, as an older and wiser man, he knew that his message was going to be equally unpalatable. There was no easy 'yes and'. He couldn't say 'Yes, carry on as you are, God is pleased you're thinking about him and will do his best to help you in every way he can.' He knew that God's was an 'if . . . then' message rather than 'yes and'.

As far as God was concerned there was a lot the people must do before he could bless them. They first had to rid themselves of the Baals and Ashtoreths which littered their hillsides. These were Canaanite gods which had lured the people away from worship of the living God. He was not prepared to compete with man-made deities. They either believed in him totally or not at all. He demanded that the nation of Israel rid themselves and their land of such alternatives.

Samuel was determined that once the 'clean up' was finished, there was more work to do. It would be easy for

Israel to carry on in a self-righteous manner, pleased that the Ashtoreths and Baals had disappeared from the landscape, but blandly pursuing their own lives and mapping out their own futures. That was why stage two of Samuel's sermon commanded them to commit themselves to God. God had committed himself to them through history and now demanded that they should return his love by committing themselves totally to him. This led to Samuel's third point. Commitment must not be passive. Once reunited with their God they must display that marriage to the whole world through serving him. God was keen that the world should know him and Israel was a crucial part in that plan. Through their central geographical position in the world and their many mercantile links from nomadic wanderings they were expected to reflect God's glory in everything they did.

Samuel was convinced that if they showed sorrow for their sin in such a tangible way, God would definitely deliver them. Yet it was still important to mark their repentance in other visible forms. So at Mizpah the whole congregation drew water and poured it out on the ground. Many gallons hit the earth as a token of the people's desire to be totally cleansed by God. The very sight of water must have made adults and children alike think of drink and food. Samuel, however, had other ideas. It was important to spend the day thinking about and praying to God. Preparing and serving food to so many people would be a lengthy distraction for a large number of people. So he pronounced a fast in order to concentrate every mind on spiritual matters.

Meanwhile the Philistines had heard the commotion and watched the movement of countless Israelite families towards Mizpah. Their intelligence had informed them that there was a large gathering which had been there all day.

The rulers were surprised. The Israelites had given very little resistance over the past twenty years. This was an ominous sign. Perhaps they were regrouping and whipping up the people to fight the Philistines. What if they found another leader like Samson? The very mention of that name made the generals shiver. Word must be relayed quickly before the Israelites had time to organize themselves.

In the Israelite camp peace had been restored. Men and women were enjoying that warm glowing feeling which accompanies the belief that God has accepted the penitent. Samuel was in the middle of another stirring speech. God had been far away from the people over the past two decades, but that was because of their rebellion. Now they had repented, he would bless and deliver them from all their enemies. He had said this at the beginning of the day. But it was good to hear it again. Play it again Samuel, again and again. It had become almost a catch phrase 'The Lord will deliver you from the hand of the Philistines.' The people 'oohed' and 'aahed' their approval. They smiled at each other and agreed this was the kind of message they needed to hear and Samuel was the type of leader they wanted.

It wasn't long before the 'oohing' and 'aahing' turned from grunts of pleasure to groans of fear. Someone brought word that the Philistines were ready to attack and would be at Mizpah at any moment.

Faith is always easy in the abstract. When Samuel talked about 'enemies' and the 'Philistines' it all seemed so far away. It was easy to feel confident surrounded by so many like-minded children of God. Suddenly the abstract enemy was a reality. They were pounding towards Mizpah and very shortly would be attacking man, woman and child. Faith was not quite so easy in the middle of such a crisis.

Samuel calmed the rising fears by offering a young lamb

as a sacrifice to God. It was important to remind the people that their confidence for the ensuing battle rested on the fact that they were now in a right relationship with God. So Samuel put into practice what he had been saying all day and pleaded with God to deliver them.

Samuel knew that God would deliver, but had no idea how he would do it. Not once did he hazard a guess at the nature of God's deliverance; he merely affirmed its certainty. His hope was not based on prowess as a soldier. Unlike Jephthah, Gideon, Samson and Barak he never once led the people into battle. His only weapon was prayer and so on behalf of his people he asked God to intervene.

The intervention was spectacular. Using the ploy which had worked so well against Sisera, God opened the heavens and the Philistines were suddenly in the middle of an almighty thunder storm. The crashing of thunder claps sent the horses into a panic. The heavy rain turned the ground into a quagmire and mud clogged the wheels of the chariots. The soldiers were frightened by the zigzag lightning cracking the sky. The whole Philistine army was thrown into total disarray. The Israelites saw their plight and moved in quickly and easily to secure a memorable victory.

After the euphoria had died down, Samuel reassembled the Israelites. They must be reminded that all the elements of the day were linked. They had rid their land of Ashtoreths, sought God's forgiveness and defeated the enemy. It was one continuous line of despair, repentance and deliverance. So Samuel erected a stone monument of the battle. He called it Ebenezer. The very name ('stone of help') would remind the people that Ebenezer had been the scene of many defeats at the hand of Philistines. Was Samuel wryly preaching another sermon?

The theme would have been something along the lines

that when we repent, God is willing to turn our area of defeat into one of victory.

Who's in charge?

On that day the people learnt to put their trust in God the deliverer; the deliverer who was certain to deliver, yet unpredictable in the actual way he would act. It wasn't long, however, before Israel forgot every lesson God had taught them through Samuel at Mizpah. As well as the Philistines, the Ammonites were a constant source of annoyance to the Israelites. Nahash their king prepared to come up against them. In a state of panic, they decided Samuel was getting older and might not be with them much longer. How could they face the enemy, when the spiritual leader might disappear off the face of the earth? What if, in the middle of a battle, the excitement got too great and he had a massive cardiac arrest, leaving the Israelites easy prey for the enemy? There was always Joel or Abijah, Samuel's two sons. But they were as despised as Hophni and Phinehas had been before them. It was well known they didn't come anywhere near Samuel in terms of spirituality. It was common knowledge they accepted bribes and freed some wealthy people who should have been severely punished.

The people began to agree that they needed a new leader. Why not find a king? Then they would be like most of the other nations. Whenever the Ammonites or Philistines prepared to attack, they'd have a king ready to champion the forces and a militia on stand by. This would prevent the normal panic of rooting around for people who would come to Israel's aid, and waiting for God to raise up a leader. Whilst they were on the subject of God, they liked the idea of him stepping in with stage-managed thunderstorms, but found it all too unpredictable. They never knew what he was going to do next or when he was going to do it. It had been exciting, but, with hindsight, perhaps it had been a little nerve-wracking. So they wanted a little bit of predictability in national affairs. From now on a king was the thing. They would break the news to Samuel and ask him to appoint a monarch over Israel.

Samuel was understandably upset. They people were forgetting that Israel's one experiment with kingship had been disastrous. Abimelech, Gideon's son, had not liked his father's words when he rejected the offers of the people to make him their king. Gideon had said 'I will not rule over you, and my son will not rule over you: the Lord will rule over you.' Abimelech wasn't too keen on unpredictability either, so he got himself appointed as king at Shechem. His reign of terror began with wiping out seventy of Gideon's relatives, in case they had eyes on the newly-established throne. The terror didn't last long, however, and his reign ended as ingloriously as it had begun, with a lady dropping a millstone on his neck.

Samuel was afraid a new kingship would create similar problems to those of Abimelech's reign. He was also fully aware that the people were seeking a king so that they could be like the other nations. Yet the distinguishing feature of Israel up to now had been that they were unlike every other nation. No other country could boast a God who was so active and powerful in national affairs. Israel's *raison d'être* was in danger of being destroyed to meet the whims of certain outspoken people.

Samuel's diappointment was no doubt also personal. He had never cheated any Israelite or taken anybody's ox or donkey. As he thought about kingship he remembered all the horror stories he'd heard about kings of other nations. Any king of Israel would certainly be the same. The pro-monarchists believed that the king would give them so much. Samuel knew that what little he gave would be cancelled by what he took from the people. They would lose their children in the service of the king and quite possibly their land. They would also have to pay heavy taxes to maintain the new monarchy. So they were turning from Samuel, who had taken nothing, to a king who would legitimately take everything. Even more sinister was the fact they were moving from a God who delighted to give, to a king who would drain the nation's resources.

God featured greatly in Samuel's sermons on the monarchy. He reminded the people that throughout Israel's history they had cried to the Lord in great distress and he had always delivered them, provided their repentance had been genuine. The way he delivered had always been unexpected. He had sent Moses, Gideon, Barak, Jephthah and even Samuel himself. To prove his point in the middle of this particular sermon, Samuel called on God to send thunder and rain. That would be something, as it was wheat harvest time, a period normally free of heavy rainfall. The rains and thunder duly came. Samuel interpreted the deluge as proof of God's displeasure at the people appointing a king. It was also proof that an unexpected God was not the same as an unreliable God. If only they called whenever they were in distress, God would hear them.

Samuel challenges Saul
A frightened leader

Saul had assembled a fair-sized army. Two thousand men were with him and another thousand with his son Jonathan. Jonathan's detachment successfully attacked the Philistine outpost at Geba. It was time for the trumpets to sound.

Saul lost no time in organizing the fanfare and sending the message through Israel. Using his kingly licence, the message read 'Saul has attacked the Philistine outpost, and now Israel has become an offence to the Philistines.' After all Jonathan was younger than he. The dispatch went on to invite Israelite men to join Saul at Gilgal ready for the next sortie against the hated enemy.

Saul and his men waited for seven days at Gilgal. At the end of that period, Samuel was expected to come and lead Israel in devotions and sacrifice an animal on their behalf. As the time went on the people became frightened and started to leave Saul. The Philistines were massing at Michmash. It was near enough for the Hebrews to hear what was happening. News was relayed through Saul's camp that the Philistines had three-thousand chariots and at least that number of soldiers. Saul did not have the spiritual poise to encourage the troops. Why didn't he remind them what God had done at Ebenezer? Or what he had recently done through Jonathan? Instead, Saul sat waiting for Samuel; he's the spiritual one, when he comes everything will be alright.

Saul's lack of spiritual insight is a proof of what Samuel had predicted. Israel were now on their own. They had put all their faith in a man and excluded God. Although Samuel had promised that if king and people sought God's forgiveness he would lead them, at Gilgal there was no such pact. Saul had no hope to offer the people and as the minutes ticked into hours and hours moved into days, the soldiers started to disappear. They didn't fancy being sitting-ducks for fast-moving Philistine charioteers. They took their destiny into their own hands and fled into the hills.

At the end of seven days, Saul's army had dwindled from two thousand to six hundred. The odds had changed from one against two Philistines to one against ten. Saul himself now joined the panic. He was incapable of encouraging the people as Samuel had done at Mizpah. There is no 'The Lord will deliver us' speech for the people. Only the sight of their new regent quaking with fear, waiting for Samuel.

Eventually, Saul decided he had waited long enough. He took the burnt offering and offered it to God. Just as he was finishing the ceremony, Samuel arrived. It was this which led to the first confrontation between the two men. Samuel, consecrated as the priest, was furious that Saul had taken upon himself the God-given role of priest.

'You acted foolishly. You have not kept the command the Lord your God gave you.' The words were spilling out of Samuel. He ended his tirade by telling Saul that his kingdom would not endure. God was going to give the kingdom to someone else. It would be a person who was much more 'after God's own heart'.

This was not the only argument between the two men. Later they were to have a far more serious disagreement and one which resulted in Samuel never seeing Saul again. It followed God's command via Samuel that Saul and his troops should utterly destroy the Amalekites and wipe out every remembrance of them. Saul failed to carry out the commands totally and spared the life of the king and also allowed his soldiers to help themselves to loot. This was the final straw for Samuel and proved, once and for all, that Saul had total disregard for God's word.

God challenges Samuel (1 Samuel 16)

Samuel had been going through a long period of despair. Daily he mourned over the disaster of Saul. The Amalekite incident had been the final episode in a sordid tale of mistakes and inadequacy. He had stayed out of Saul's way from then on and allowed him to carry on making a sorry mess of running the country.

It was during one of these lengthy periods of feeling sorry for himself that God had told Samuel in no uncertain terms to stop mourning. He had a job for him. He wanted him to go to Bethlehem and secretly anoint the future king. Understandably he did not relish the thought. What if Saul found out? Surely he'd try to kill him. Eventually and reluctantly he went.

Which one Lord?

Samuel knew that one of the sons of Jesse of Bethlehem was to be the future king. But he didn't know which one. Jesse decided to help matters along by starting at the top. If he brought the best out first, that could save the whole morning and it would prevent the other brothers from becoming too involved in the 'Who's going to make it to number one' race. They could all amicably congratulate their brother and look forward to the time when he'd be crowned publicly. So contestant number one was brought on. Eliab was Jesse's favourite. He was tall, good looking and sensible. This was the one. Just as he was going to mouth is approval, he felt a terrible rebuke from God. 'Don't consider his appearance or his height,' he said, 'for I have rejected him. The Lord does not look at the things man looks at. Man looks at the outward appearance, but the Lord looks at the heart.' Samuel had no alternative but to say 'Sorry. Can we have the next, please.'

So they did. And the next and the next and the next . . . until they'd got through the lot. Poor Samuel. Had he misunderstood God's message? They'd have to have a re-run. How embarrassing. It was time for a nervous cough.

'Are these all the sons you have?' he asked Jesse.

Well, there was another. The youngest. A bit of a dreamer. Always playing his flute. Writing poems and trying to get them to rhyme when he should be eating his meal. Hardly monarchy material. Jesse hadn't even considered him worthy of the starting line. After God's rebuke Samuel had no alternative but to demand that Jesse sent for him. As soon as he came in God was active again. he left Samuel in no doubt that this was his choice.

Samuel had almost forgotten that decisions based on human criteria had brought so many problems to Israel. The Israelites had chosen Saul mainly because he was taller than everyone else and extremely handsome. His imposing presence had lured them into appointing him as their leader. Yet Samuel had lived with the disastrous consequences of that decision. He had almost made a similar mistake with Eliab. God had caught him just in time.

It is ironic that Samuel, whose life of faith had begun as a young inexperienced boy, was in danger of neglecting another, simply because of his youthfulness. All men of faith need such reminders. It is easy from the pedestal of wisdom and advancing years to reject other Christians who show the very traits they once possessed. Traits which God transformed from weakness into strength.

The faith of a child

So far, our heroes have all expressed manly traits. Samson ripped open a lion with his bare hands and young David slew the feared giant with a sling and a stone. Even Gideon and Barak, the two nervous members of our fraternity, eventually mustered enough confidence to lead Israel against their hated enemies, whilst Jephthah rallied the troops to defeat the Ammonites. It is interesting that the compiler of Hebrews should place Samuel towards the end of his list. Samuel's first act of faith for God was expressed as an untutored youngster in contrast to the adult bravado of the others. His very presence in the list must challenge modern Christians in their understanding of faith as it relates to their attitude to children. So often our attitude is similar to that of the minister who on his day off was laying a concrete path outside his manse. His children were happily playing with the youngsters from next door. Suddenly, against his commands, they ran excitedly down the path, leaving footprints embedded in the still drying concrete. Realizing what had happened, he shouted at the children at the top of his voice. Hearing the commotion, his next door neighbour came to the fence.

'Hmm,' he snorted, 'thought you were a man of God. Loving little children and all that. Call yourself a Christian?'

'Listen,' said the minister, 'I love children in the abstract but can't stand them in the concrete.'

As Christians it is so easy to keep our concepts of children in the abstract compartment. Yes, of course God loves them. Certainly Jesus died for them on the cross and he wants them to come to him. But when it comes to practical faith, we don't rate them very highly. It is so easy for our attitude towards faith to be shaped by modern society. As modern business celebrates trouble-shooting executives who soar to the top of their ladders, so Christians can sometimes encourage a faith which bravely goes where others fear to tread. There is little room for tremulous and troublesome children in such a scenario. Samuel's story therefore brings us down to earth with a bump. Throughout the breadth of Israel there must surely have been a God-fearing man who could have carried the message of judgment. Instead, God chooses a young boy who has very little knowledge of the living God.

As we consider practical faith, it is vital we pause to discuss the implications of this fact. All the men we have studied have only succeeded as they discovered a childlike trust in God. Once they lost that, it led to the problems of Gideon who ended up worshipping an ephod, of David who slipped down a path of sensuous gratification and of Samson who satisfied his lust for vengeance. For Jesus and for Bible writers, one of the hallmarks of true faith was childlike humility, a humility Samuel possessed as a child and expressed throughout his adult ministry.

In the world of Jesus, religion was often associated with power and intellect. The Zealots were a religious group who believed the only hope for the Israelite nation was through the power of the sword. The Pharisees, at the other end of the scale, had found six hundred and thirteen laws which had to be memorized and kept assiduously. This was clearly no world for children. Both popular visions celebrated attributes they did not possess; political power, moral purity and intellectual ability. Some Jews even claimed that if every Jew kept all six hundred and thirteen laws on any given Sabbath, then the Messiah would appear. For such a proposition to work, they had to exclude certain people from the reckoning. These were tax collectors, prostitutes and children.

It is against this backcloth that the words of Jesus are to be understood when he placed a child in the middle of his circle of followers and said 'Whoever humbles himself like this child is the greatest in the kingdom of heaven' (Matthew 18:4). These words were uttered after James and John had argued about who should be the greatest in the kingdom of God. Jesus was underlining the fact that faith begins with childlike humility.

Whilst all children will sometime or other drive their parents to distraction with their conceit and braggish claims, one of the hallmarks of childhood is acceptance. It is remarkable how after a child is reprimanded she will not nurse resentment but carry on in the family circle as if nothing had happened. Perhaps it was this aspect of humility Jesus had in mind. He was challenging James and John and the other disciples to reconsider the way they harboured resentment for each other over the question of greatness in the kingdom. Our high view of ourselves in comparison with others can often get in the way of an uninhibited life of faith. It can lead us down all kinds of *cul-de-sacs* and we can expend energy trying to justify ourselves instead of working for God's kingdom.

As we realize our smallness in comparison with God, we will be prepared to be controlled and corrected by him. The writer to the Hebrews informs us that, like a father, God chides those whom he loves. As I nurture this childlike view of myself, then my life of faith will develop according to God's wishes rather than my own.

The humility of a child does not only apply to his attitude to correction. It also carries over into the realm of wonder. There is nothing to beat the wide-eyed expression of a child opening an unexpected Christmas present. In the spiritual realm children often express the same sense of wonder.

A little girl was being given her first Bible instruction from her grandmother. The old lady was reading the story of creation from a children's Bible. After a while she paused and asked the child 'Well, what do you think of it so far?' 'Oh I love it. You never know what God is going to do next. It's so exciting.'

It is this wonder which the psalmist celebrates in the eighth psalm. In the midst of a magnificent poem in praise of God's majestic rule over the heavens and the earth, he says 'from the lips of children and infants you have ordained praise'. Surrounded by stars and galaxies which celebrate God's name, the writer imagines children uttering their sense of wonder without the clutter of theological jargon. They really do feel 'wow' and so they express it.

Our men of faith had that same childlike wonder and trust at different points of their stories. Gideon, clothed with the Holy Spirit was able to blow the trumpet and rally the troops. As old age crept up on him, he lost that humility and dependency on God and began to satisfy his own desires of the flesh.

It is interesting to note that Samuel kept his childlike faith throughout his life. At his divine call, God informed him he 'was going to do something in Israel'. Although that particular message was one of doom, Samuel kept this vision of a national God throughout his ministry. He never allowed Jehovah to become parochial but always encouraged the whole nation to repent and see what God could do.

We have already seen that Samuel prevented the people from ever feeling they could manipulate God. They must expect him to work but never anticipate what he was going to do or how he was going to do it. This is a hallmark of childlike wonder and it stayed with Samuel throughout his ministry.

The words of Jesus that unless we become as little children we will never see the kingdom of faith must not be restricted just to the beginning of our pilgrimages of faith. They are words which must apply throughout our Christian experience so that, like Samuel's, our faith will remain vibrant and dependent on God.

CHAPTER EIGHT

ONE FAITH, MANY FAILURES

Climbing a hill can be tiring and soul destroying. Each step becomes a greater effort than the previous one. The body aches for relief and the mind cries for the end of the walk. At such a moment it can be helpful to look down (provided of course you're not perched precariously on a dangerous ridge). Then you will see how far you have come. That can make the whole exercise worthwhile and inspire you on to the summit.

In our study of six men of the Old Testament it would be easy to feel depressed. The failure of neurotic Gideon and sensuous David have haunted us through our study of faith. Whilst on one level we find such mistakes an encouragement to our feeble Christian life, on another they can be hugely disappointing. If those people failed, what hope is there for me? And if they have failed, what is the point of us even trying to fulfil Christ's commands and follow him?

As if anticipating such a response, the writer to the Hebrews furbishes his account of the six characters with a catalogue of their great achievements. Victories won by people who failed again and again. He is using the mountaineering technique! We mustn't despair, but rather press on, inspired by this motley company of ordinary men who let God down several times, but finally allowed him to triumph through them and produce lives of faith which have become beacons to countless generations of Christians.

On the victory side *(Hebrews 11:32–35)*

It was such men who conquered kingdoms which had subdued the Israelites for many generations. The Philistines, Midianites and Canaanites all had lengthy periods of military supremacy. They cruelly and mercilessly controlled the dispirited Israelites in such a way that release seemed impossible, even to the most optimistic Israelite. Yet, in the midst of national and political darkness, God raised up men like Gideon, Barak, Samson, Jephthah, David and Samuel to rally the nation and destroy the oppressor.

Each act of deliverance was followd by all six men judging the nation and 'administering justice'. This in a nation which frequently lost its way. Each of the six came to prominence at a time when Israel was bereft of leadership. The people frequently felt that God no longer listened to their prayers and they knew what it was to live in a society where social norms and standards were being constantly eroded. Through the help of God, each man brought a brief glimpse of the serenity that comes from a society bound together by God's word. Some, such as Samuel and David were clearly more successful than others in achieving this, yet all of them, in different ways, managed to gain the author of Hebrew's praise for their ability in administering justice.

Their victorious faith was not restricted to governmental abilities. Samson and David both proved faith could extend to power over the animal kingdom. In fact, David's youthful faith emanated from the fact that he had slain a lion and a bear whilst tending his father's sheep. Samson's prowess, although far more flamboyant and unnecessary, extended to slaying lions, foxes and donkeys.

Such faith expressed itself not only in facing wild animals undaunted, but also the sword. Time and again they all escaped the edge of the sword. If David had thought about the implications of his confrontation with Goliath he would never have gone to fight. Nor would Barak as he looked down the hill at the waiting Sisera and his chariots; nor Gideon with his divinely decimated army of three hundred men. Yet they all allowed their new-found faith to flourish in the face of growing danger. It flourished because they all expected their faith to be stretched to the limits. As they allowed that process, they discovered that their faith grew.

Faith on the move

Not one of our gallery of six had a faith that was static. All of them were told to go from where they lived, rally the Israelites, then attack the foe.

The writer to the Hebrews, describing other Old Testament characters, sees this idea of movement as crucial to faith. Abraham and Moses are both described in some detail. Abraham was prepared to leave the security of the Ur of the Chaldees for a land he knew nothing about. Moses took a similar risk in rejecting life in an Egyptian palace for the rigours of leading several thousand Israelites through the desert. It was not merely obedience to the divine call which inspired Abraham and Moses. Both were visionaries who saw beyond reality to what life could be like if God

144

were allowed to work. The promise of God that he would be the father of a nation as vast as the stars in the sky, must have sounded wildly ludicrous to friends and colleagues of Abraham. It was this vision that inspired Abraham to go, despite the slight problem of his advancing years and the fact that Sarah was well past child-bearing age.

Similarly, Moses must constantly have been inspired by the hope of what could be, rather than by reality. The desert exodus was littered with disease, rebellion and groans against his leadership, from the people and his co-leaders, Aaron and Mirian. So committed was he to the vision of the promised land, he continued against all the odds.

The odds were also stacked high against Noah, another person complimented by the author of Hebrews for his visionary faith. On bright sunny afternoons, it must have been difficult to stand by his God given vision that soon the earth would be covered with water and that the monstrous contraption in his backyard, called for some reason an ark, would be extremely useful.

The six warriors we have studied also had this visionary dimension to their faith. All called by God at a time when the future looked bleak, they believed that through the help of God there would be a time when their country would be rid of the oppressor. That is why they were prepared to go when God commanded and why they were able to convince other Israelites to join them.

Churches are often filled with Christians who have lost the element of risk in their Christian lives. In a society where the riskiest thing some people do is to move from one house to the next, the Christian church needs to rediscover the dynamic of their 'calling' God. Such a God is often too uncomfortable for suburban security. He is the God who appears in both testaments calling Abraham and

Barak to leave their homes and through Christ telling fishermen to leave their nets.

The trauma of taking such risks is more than compensated by the fact that God grants to such risk-takers a vision of what he can do. Such visions are often low down on the agendas of church meetings or parochial church councils. The equivalent of Mr Noah asking a group of deacons for permission to park his ark on the church forecourt would send shivers down most hierarchical spines. Instead churches play it safe, with budgets, sociological studies on the area intended for evangelism and projected articles on the future year. The person of vision is often mistrusted or ignored. Fortunately the men of faith we have considered were eventually heard by the Israelites. Church congregations and minsters need to encourage modern people of faith to express their God-given visions. Such visions must be tested, but before they can be tested they must be heard. If more were heard, perhaps we would see more of a dynamic evangelistically-minded church in the West, rather than one which courts safety and traditionalism.

There is, of course, always the danger of assuming that such faith will be found only in exceptionally gifted people. As if we needed reminding, Gideon and company expose such a fallacy. To underline the point, the writer of Hebrews reminds us that their faith was the result of God transforming their weakness into strength.

Men of failure? *(Hebrews 11:35–39)*

The faith we have considered has been of the sabre rattling variety. It killed lions, quenched fires, stared soldiers in the face and did not flinch at the sight of bared swords. In modern terms it is a faith for neon lights and best-selling books. Gideon, Samson and the rest would be chauffeur driven through the provinces, whisked from one filled hall to the next, to tell their 'remarkable stories'.

We all know, however, that not everyone's faith works out like that. Indeed, the writer of Hebrews concludes his section by giving just as much space to a group of people who, by contemporary standards, might be considered failures. Far from escaping the sword they end up being killed by it. Far from displaying a faith bristling with stength, they are publicly jeered and flogged. Instead of conquering kingdoms and following up militaristic feats by administering justice, they end their days out of the public eye, wandering in deserts and mountains and hiding in caves and holes in the ground. The writer, casting an eye back over Maccabean history, remembers that that period, far from being characterized by swashbuckling judges, was peopled by individuals who suffered greatly for God. Some were stoned, some were even sawn in two and many were put to death by the sword.

Such people are not paraded as failures. They are not tucked into the last section of the author's eulogy on men of faith, with an embarrassed scrawl. Far from it. They are placed side by side the flamboyant six. 'These were all,' he writes, 'commended for their faith.'

The man who in his life leads scores of people to faith in Christ is often greatly applauded. So is the woman who has triumphed over terminal illness and written countless books explaining her faith in Christ the healer. The wife who for thirty years found her husband's antagonism to Christianity kept her in the house and prevented her from playing a major part in the local fellowship, is not so highly praised. In God's eyes, all are to be commended. All have lived for a reality other than they find in the world. In their own ways they have both been moving to that city which is not of this world, whose founder and builder is God.

Failure of a different kind

Our six men all failed in different ways, yet their failure was in some way due to their own inadequacy. Gideon could not keep his God-given sense of the Holy Spirit's vibrancy and spirituality alive in his old age. Samson let himself, God and Israel down by failing to control his raging temper. Jephthah saw his daughter killed because of his own rash promise and his failure to understand the true character of God. Barak did not experience the total blessing of God because of his failure to respond immediately to the divine command. David saw his own kingdom begin to crumble because of his sin against Bathsheba and Uriah, whilst Samuel's hesitancy led to problems in the kingdom of Israel.

Our understanding of failure, so far, has been limited to this sense of making mistakes and suffering spiritually or physically as a result. Yet for many Christians, failure is something they feel as they review their Christian experience. This is failure of a different kind; failure according to the high expectations of other Christians, brought about by the failings of their own personality or intellectual inability. They have not committed murder or adultery, yet through their own shortcomings they feel inadequate. Other Christians intimidate rather than help them and they feel they have let God down.

Robert has grown up in the church youth-fellowship. At sixteen he took his 'O' levels along with eight other members of the fellowship. Now, two years on he has just re-sat them for the third time. His total haul is only two passes. Greg got ten at the first attempt and Beverley (whom he has always liked but never had the courage to court) had nine passes, all at 'A' grade. The rest of his church peer-group have now sat their 'A' level exams and all did well. Beverley is off to Oxford next September and Greg to Cambridge. Robert has been told by his tutor in the tech that there will be no place for him next academic term. His parents, who have scrimped and saved to let him re-sit his exams, have also said he must now find a job. Since June he has spent three months visiting the city employment offices, but all to no avail. He has been for seven interviews, and although all the people were extremely nice he has not had the joy of finding work.

From September he is going to be alone in the church and it is highly unlikely that any of his friends will return to his home church. Although he's not looking forward to that prospect, he has to admit that, at the moment, he feels slightly isolated from the rest of the group. In the after-eight meeting on a Sunday evening, Greg, Beverley and the others find it easy to talk about deep issues. Last Sunday Greg wanted to know what the Christian attitude to monetarist economic policy should be. Beverley waded in with her views on ahimsa or something or other, which she'd read about in some book on Eastern philosophies. Robert spent the entire hour embarrassed, clutching his praise book and waiting for Barry the leader to strum the guitar. He didn't speak for the whole session and just to make matters worse, Beverley asked him in front of all the others whether he was feeling alright.

Robert loves the Lord but finds it difficult to express his faith like the others. He reads his Bible every day and finds it fairly easy to pray by himself. But when he's in the group, if Barry asks him to lead in prayer he begins to stammer. Besides, when it comes to discussion on the Bible he can't remember verses and their references, like the others. Last year the Sunday-nighters ran an evangelistic coffee-bar in the town. Just thinking about that last night makes him shudder. He'll never forget the deep desire for the floor to open up and swallow him when Greg unexpectedly asked him to give his testimony. Robert seemed to freeze, run a temperature, stammer, dry up and shake all at the same time.

Although Robert is very happy at home and his parents are tremendously supportive, he feels he has failed. He has failed them; failed the youth group in his inability to share his faith the way they do and to discuss the Bible in a deep and relaxed manner; ultimately he feels he has failed the Lord. Surely he wants him to be dynamic and able to evangelize his neighbourhood.

Robert's story is repeated all over Britain. It is resticted neither to young people nor to males. Christians of all ages, both male and female often feel this sense of failure in their Christian lives. Whereas the failure of our six biblical characters could be corrected, there is no easy solution for the failure of people like Robert. Gideon can be encouraged to replace his temerity and inferiority with the Spirit of God's strength. In the same way Barak's hesitancy, Samson's flippancy, Jephthah's rashness, David's sensuality and Samuel's caution can all be changed into the strength of God, through the work of his spirit and application of biblical principles. What can we suggest for people like Robert?

Coping with this type of failure can often be more difficult than dealing with the failure we have already studied. If we have committed adultery like David, and our Christian life is full of failure, then it is obvious what is wrong. The problem with Robert-style failure is that it is less than obvious. It is also a problem which permeates every element of our personalities so that we do not feel worthy of serving God or capable of attempting tasks for him. Like Robert, we compare ourselves with other Christians in the church and feel that we are abject failures.

When Jesus was on earth he made a point of seeking out society's rejects. Whilst it could be argued that prostitutes and tax collectors were failures because of their own sin, he did deal with many more who were considered failures through no fault of their own. The paralysed man who is described in Mark's gospel, is a classic example of a person in this category. To his friends and no doubt to himself, his only major problem was one of physical paralysis. Jesus looks beyond the externals and claims that for this man what is important is that God deals with the paralysis of sin. It is for this reason he is able to say that the most important statement for him is not 'take up your bed and walk' but 'your sins are forgiven you'. This story teaches us a lot about failure and Jesus' attitude to it. It is as though he is saying, if I healed you on the outside and you walked around paralysed internally, maimed in your attitude to God and spiritual truth, I wouldn't have done you any favours. So, he first heals him internally and then as a public demonstration that he is now spiritually walking, he speaks the word of command and the man is physically cured. As far as the onlookers were concerned, the biggest failure in this man's life was his physical disability. Jesus' response underlines his disagreement with the popular analysis.

Translating this truth into Robert's story turns the situation upside down. His peer group saw success in terms of good examination results, an interesting job, an ability to sparkle in public and an intellectual capability to shine. On all four counts Robert missed the mark and was considered a failure. According to Jesus' preaching on success and failure, the most vital part of Robert's life is his soul. Jesus underlined this point when he told his audience they should pay as much attention to their souls as they do to their bodies.

Our society locates success in the realm of the body. It is body-conscious and encourages any man or woman who wishes to succeed to have a similar view. The body is to be housed, clothed, massaged, sunbathed, trimmed, slimmed, exercised, built up, cared for and a thousand and one other things. The man who can do most or all of these well is considered a success by society. The same energy is not extended to the soul. Yet the thrust of Jesus' preaching is that if we are a failure according to our body-conscious society, it doesn't matter. The question is has our soul been cared for? Such teaching is not a sentimental attempt to make the most of a bad job for people such as Robert. Rather it seems to be at the heart of Jesus' gospel preaching.

When he talked with the woman of Samaria, Jesus reiterated the same point. Although her failure was partly of her own making, he knew that her attempts at success and happiness had been solely in the physical realm. Five men had serviced her carnal appetite yet she was still unsatisfied. Jesus offered her, as he offered the paralytic, a life full of internal success in a body which had tasted only failure. Jesus promised 'Whoever drinks the water I give him will never thirst. Indeed, the water I give him will become in him a spring of water welling up to eternal life.' This is success as Jesus saw it. To the world it is failure, but to Christians who feel stricken by a materialistic world they are words of music and hope. For all the Roberts in every Christian union and church these words form the filter though which success and failure must be judged.

CHAPTER NINE

A MINISTER LOOKS·AROUND

He had looked at the membership list four times. Every time he hoped that a new name would leap up and suggest itself to him. He was looking for three new deacons. His church had a history of female deacons, so it did not matter whether they were male or female. Even with that latitude, the minister could not say he had three definite names. True, the piece of paper next to the half-emptied coffee-cup had been scribbled on six times. The names, though, were more an expression of hope than certainty. They all had strengths, which was why they had found their way on to the piece of paper, yet they also had terrible weaknesses.

George Harris sometimes stood in for the minister in a prayer meeting. He was a fairly popular, unassuming sort of person. Unfortunately, he was terribly unsure of himself. Many times, just before a prayer meeting, the minister had received a phone call. It was George, wondering whether he really was the right man to lead the meeting. There were far better people in the fellowship, why hadn't the minister asked them? Besides, George had read his talk three times and in his opinion, it was dreadful rubbish. Could the minister step in for him and he would stay at home, look after the children and give Brenda a chance to go to the meeting. The minister knew this speech off by heart – he had heard it so many times. No. George wouldn't do. A good fellow to have around, but not leadership material.

Brian Simmonds seemed to suffer from similar problems to George. In fact, George was possibly more dynamic than Brian. If George had been given the 'red pen' treatment where did that leave Brian? He was a steady plodder, but terribly low-key. Although he had ability, he didn't seem able to express it completely. The minister recalled how on one occasion he had asked Brian to speak to the young people's group on a Sunday evening. He had been amazed to arrive late and find Brian sitting in the corner, all smiles, listening to his wife's exposition on Luke 9. Susan was a formidable person. A strong-headed, hard-hitting Christian who seemed to have all the answers for all of life's problems. Many of the congregation found her difficult to accept. The trouble with approaching Brian about the diaconate was that a vote for him would mean a vote for Susan. The red pen had no hesitation and moved on to the next entry.

Simon Robertson was the youngest of the six names on the piece of paper. In his early twenties, he was a burly athlete. Renowned as an excellent rugby player, he was a great favourite with the girls. Since he had been in charge of the young people's work, the number had increased dramatically (both male and female!).

Simon had a tremendous gift for speaking at young-people's events. His talks were always lively, full of illustrations and humour. Unfortunately, Simon's temper matched his physique. He was extremely volatile and had been known to throw out unwanted members of the youth group. This temper also expressed itself verbally and he had mortally offended Mrs Crabtree in a famous church meeting which almost ended in a fight between her eldest son and Simon. Thinking about that incident, the minister recalled at least two occasions when Simon had been extremely rude to him. It was clearly time for the red pen. Besides, Simon was much bigger than the minister!

He peered at the next name. Janice Green. She was a good Christian, very devout and a tremendous student of the Word. He remembered how on many occasions at prayer meetings he had struggled to recall a biblical reference. She was always the first to supply chapter and verse. She would certainly be an asset on the diaconate. No doubt she would support him in his desire to introduce more in-depth study into the church.

Unfortunately Janice had one huge problem. It wasn't really her fault, yet it was a problem she could never overcome. None of the newcomers to the church knew anything about it. The older people, however, knew all the sordid details. Although they kept it to themselves, they would surely oppose her appointment as a deacon. New families assumed her mother was a widow. Older families knew otherwise. Besides, any mention of Janice's name in connection with the diaconate would only rake up the past. It would be difficult for the younger deacons who knew nothing about it and any mention of her illegitimacy would only cause unpleasantness for Janice. So reluctantly, more out of a concern for her than anyone else, he crossed out her name.

Dan Davies' problems were even worse than Janice's. He had preached many times on a Sunday, always powerfully and acceptably to every member of the congregation. It was only six months ago that a visitor had shared Dan's story with the minister. Amazed to find him in such a prominent position in the church, the visitor, who knew Dan well from a previous church, had made an appointment to see the minister after evening worship. It transpired that Muriel, Dan's wife, was in fact his second wife. She had been pregnant with Dan's child whilst she was married to Reg, a respected deacon in their church. Before the birth of the child, Reg had been killed in a car accident and there had even been some questions raised at the inquest whether Dan had tampered with the vehicle (unfounded, but of course the mud had stuck). A mere three months after the tragedy, Dan had married Muriel, much to the dismay of the fellowship.

As the minister looked at Dan's name, he felt again the anger on first hearing this story. In his subsequent chat with Dan, he had been impressed by the depth of his repentance. Dan had not mentioned the saga, because he had felt totally forgiven and cleansed from sin. Although nobody else knew any details, the minister was afraid someone would find out. So the red pen swooped down on the page.

The name Stephen Saunders took him into much calmer waters. Stephen had been deacon in a previous church. He was an excellent preacher. The sort to rally dispirited troops, although the minister had to admit that sometimes his expostion was slightly naive. He was heavily committed to the idea of God being in control of every aspect of the church's life. This led him to criticize an over-interest in organization. The minster felt such a stance was fine for the pulpit, but not so encouraging for business meetings. Still that was a minor point.

Not such a minor point were Stephen's children. John and Alan were both in their twenties. John had actually served a short prison sentence for deception. Alan was self-employed, but was renowned in the community for his shady business deals. The minister thought for a moment. Wasn't there a verse somewhere about deacons being able to manage their children? That was sure to be mentioned at the church meeting. Anyway, in addition to his children, Stephen had often shown that he did not like confrontation. That was not a good trait for a potential deacon. Yet, he was a godly man. The red pen hovered and hit the page as two large question marks.

The minister was now at the end of his list. He had five thick lines and two large question marks. He had often preached on Hebrews 11, but had clearly missed the application. He failed to see that Gideon was in his congregation in the guise of George. He was also unaware that Israel had coped with Brian's problems in the shape of Barak. God had allowed him to go with Deborah and used him in spite of his dependence on her. He also failed to realize that Simon was a saint in comparison with Samson, yet God had persevered and through him gained a notable victory over the Philistine god Dagon and his devotees. The minister's sensitivity about Janice's background failed to do justice to God's choosing of Jephthah. His similar sensitivity to Dan Davies also appears incredible in the light of God's use of David in the Old Testament, and Samuel's influence over Israel questions his marks next to the name of Stephen Saunders.

The minister failed to realize that men and women of faith will also be prone to failure. He also failed to see that if their mistakes are confessed before God, He will help their faith to grow through each responsibility they are given.

We have not named the church or the minister, because they are purely a figment of imagination . . . Or are they?

List of Bible passages used

Gideon: Judges 6–8
Barak: Judges 4–5
Samson: Judges 13–16
Jephthah: Judges 11
David: 1 Samuel 18, 20–23; 2 Samuel 1, 11, 27, 29;
  Psalm 32, 51
Samuel: 1 Samuel 3, 7, 16